Rediscovering the Divine

Rediscovering
the Divine

*New Ways to Understand, Experience,
and Express God*

Cyprian Consiglio,
OSB Cam.

ORBIS BOOKS
Maryknoll, New York 10545

Founded in 1970, Orbis Books endeavors to publish works that enlighten the mind, nourish the spirit, and challenge the conscience. The publishing arm of the Maryknoll Fathers and Brothers, Orbis seeks to explore the global dimensions of the Christian faith and mission, to invite dialogue with diverse cultures and religious traditions, and to serve the cause of reconciliation and peace. The books published reflect the views of their authors and do not represent the official position of the Maryknoll Society. To learn more about Maryknoll and Orbis Books, please visit our website at www.orbisbooks.com

Manufactured in the United States of America

Library of Congress Cataloging-in-Publication Data

Names: Consiglio, Cyprian, author.
Title: Rediscovering the divine : new ways to understand, experience, and
    express God / Cyprian Consiglio, OSB Cam.
Description: Maryknoll, New York : Orbis Books, 2023. | Includes
    bibliographical references. | Summary: "Consiglio challenges conceptions
    of God, inviting us experience God in a new way"—Provided by publisher.
Identifiers: LCCN 2022051197 (print) | LCCN 2022051198 (ebook) | ISBN
    9781626985070 (trade paperback) | ISBN 9781608339693 (epub)
Subjects: LCSH: Spirituality—Christianity.
Classification: LCC BV4501.3 .C6222 2023 (print) | LCC BV4501.3 (ebook) |
    DDC 248—dc23/eng/20230118
LC record available at https://lccn.loc.gov/2022051197
LC ebook record available at https://lccn.loc.gov/2022051198

Dedicated to the memories of

Bruno Barnhart, OSB Cam. (1931–2015)

Robert Hale, OSB Cam. (1937–2018)

my spiritual amma, Sr. Pascaline Coff, OSB (1927–2021)

and my beloved babbo, Salvatore I. Consiglio (1931–2021)

mentors, friends, and wisdom guides.

Contents

Introduction: An Island Is the Tip of a Mountain   1

1. Beginning and End   7

2. The Silence   22

3. Abyss and Ground   45

4. Great Mother   57

5. Word (and Wisdom) Out of Silence   69

6. Wisdom Builds Her House   85

7. Traces of Wisdom, Seeds of the Word   104

8. Sacrament of History   121

9. Thought Becomes Fire   137

10. Dynamic Energy   154

11. Participation   169

Conclusion: Everything Is Holy Now   187

Appendix: Lady Wisdom in Scripture   193

Acknowledgments   197

An Island Is the Tip of a Mountain

I spent the first twenty years of my monastic life deeply immersed in and influenced by the life and work of Bede Griffiths, OSB Cam., specifically two themes of his. One was his insistence on a tripartite anthropology, that the human person is not made up of just body and soul but is also spirit. The other was what he called the universal call to contemplation, that all people are called to share in the graces of the contemplative life, and that at the core and end of all authentic spiritual traditions there is a mystical experience.

Based on those two themes I gave countless retreats and conferences, immersed myself in the study of the meditation traditions and Asian spirituality, wrote articles and my first two books, and was deeply involved in interreligious dialogue. As a musician, I was influenced by these two themes in much of the music that I wrote and performed.

After a ten-year hiatus from living in my monastic community, during which time I did much of that work, I was asked to return and take on the role of prior. I instinctively knew that I would need to turn then to more classical Western Christian sources in my teaching within the community, and I did so with new eyes and new fervor without, however, losing that other influence. It was then that I really fell under the influence of my esteemed and erudite confrere and intellectual mentor, Fr. Bruno Barnhart, OSB Cam.

Bruno was a former prior of our community, having had to lead the brothers, oftentimes grudgingly, into the era of the Second Vatican Council. While taking on that role, he remained an autodidact of a wide range of topics stretching from literary criticism to modern poetry, and as would be expected, monastic sources and mystical theology East and West. He also edited *The One Light*, the definitive anthology of the writings of Bede Griffiths, whom he knew well.[1] Though he published only three books of his own, Bruno left behind a mountain of notes, homilies, and outlines of conferences as well as an extensive personal library. As one of our former monks said about him, "Every word he says has a thousand mirrors on it." Though not well known outside of a small (but influential) circle, I was impressed by the long list of people who made their way down the serpentine Pacific Coast Highway on the Big Sur coast to search Bruno out and spend time in his company and conversation, influential writers and great minds such as Henri Nouwen, Donald Nicholl, Raimundo Panikkar, Richard Rohr, and Richard Tarnas, along with a host of clergy, including several bishops, fellow religious, and lay people.

Bruno used to regularly invite me to be a part of some of those conversations. He also urged me to write and exhorted me to offer regular chapter conferences for the brothers when I became prior. Besides the many conversations he and I had over meals and in his cell, when I conferred with him on matters both practical and intellectual, I had the immense privilege of accompanying him closely during the final few years, months, weeks, and days of his life, hours traveling back and forth to doctors' appointments, then a hospital stay, and visits with him during an extended time in a rehabilitation facility. After we brought Bruno home for his final hours, aware that death was imminent, I sat next to his bed

---

[1] Bruno's own introductory explanatory notes for each section of that book are as precious as Bede's own writings.

during my allotted time keeping vigil, working on the homily for his funeral Mass, knowing that that task would fall to me as prior, knowing also how well known Bruno was for his scintillating and insightful preaching. For some reason I decided to re-read Bruno's book *Second Simplicity* there at his bedside, perhaps the most accessible of his works, as I kept watch while he breathed his final breaths.

It is a temptation for a homilist at a funeral to eulogize rather than preach, but that is not the task at hand. The preacher even at a funeral is tasked with preaching the Gospel of Jesus Christ, the Paschal Mystery of Jesus' life, passion, death, and resurrection. The eulogy is for another moment. There is, however, nothing to stop one from using the deceased's life as a framing device for that homily. And as I read through *Second Simplicity*, I decided to preach the "gospel according to Bruno" and share what I understood to be his unique insight into the gift of the Christ event and Christianity's specific contribution to the great conversation going on across the globe in churches, ashrams, zendos, temples, synagogues, and mosques about spirituality and the working of the Divine in our world.

When I was asked to write an article in memory of him for a monastic revue, after Bruno's death, I based it on that homily. I used that article again as the basis for a conference that I offered to a local group. That conference turned into four conferences, and within a year I had nearly a 100-page outline as it grew into a full retreat and then a twelve-part series. The topic just kept expanding in my own mind and heart. I never referred to *Second Simplicity* after the initial impetus; I simply began improvising on the themes myself. It was almost as if after twenty years of digging so deeply into the thought of Bede Griffiths, I didn't even realize that I had tapped out that root and was looking for a new vocabulary.

Bruno suggested in *Second Simplicity* that there are four poles or dimensions that manifest themselves out of the unitive experience of many ancient religious traditions. I shall also refer to them as "energies." In Christianity, these four dimensions are represented by the arms of the Cross.[2] He named those four dimensions the Silence, the Word, the Music, and the Dance. This is where we will begin. The first three of these energies, poles, or dimensions are related to the three Persons of the Holy Trinity, whom we normally refer to as the Father, the Son, and the Holy Spirit. Then there is a fourth, which is not just a person. With my late confrere, I believe that this fourth is another energy, another essential pole or dimension of Christianity that is often overlooked, unrealized, and unarticulated. We will have hints at it along the way but will really explore it in the final chapter.

Bruno was very influenced by Carl Jung, and you might recognize that the idea of quaternity was also a theme that fascinated Jung. Jung was always looking for the psychological completeness of a fourth wherever there was a trinity, always wanting to complete a triadic figure with a fourth element. All of this Jung ultimately tied in with the psychological process of individuation—and I think that's a key to this mysterious fourth element, because individuation, which you might say is the *telos*, the end, of Jungian psychoanalysis, is to bring everything from the unconscious into consciousness. That is to say, Jung thought that the Christian Trinity was at least *psychologically* incomplete, that the fourth must have been either forgotten or hidden or "displaced" in the unconscious. Simply put, the fourth element is the shadow, and although it is dark, that shadow is not just evil and not necessarily evil at all. There's also a "holy darkness," as the song goes.

Like Jung, because of this idea of the quaternity, Bruno was also attracted to mandalas, and very often when he would begin a retreat conference, he would start by drawing a cross/mandala on the whiteboard or chalkboard and then proceed to fill it in throughout his teaching. I like to think that when he died he drew one last mandala on the board, but this time he left it blank for

---

[2]Bruno Barnhart, *Second Simplicity: The Inner Shape of Christianity* (New York: Paulist Press, 1999), 4–5.

me to fill in with colors, words, and images in my own way. This book is my filling in of that blank mandala.

One last note by way of introduction. This work was originally titled "From the Ground Up" because this is what we aim to do, to rediscover the Divine and articulate our understanding of God all over again, starting from someplace new, "not in some heaven lightyears away," but in the very Ground of Being which is the ground of our own being and consciousness. Nor is it removed from the ground we stand on, the ground of Mother Earth and creation. And so this is not a theology or spirituality from the "top down" but from the "ground up."

In order to do that we may have to do some gentle and respectful deconstructing of "all imaginations and all the notions we have acquired from outside ourselves," in the words of Johannes Tauler, whom we shall encounter below. With that gentle respect in mind, I mean in no way to diminish the venerable tradition of Father, Son, and Holy Spirit. If anything, what follows is a way to increase our knowledge of these Persons.

A metaphor might help. I am tempted to use a common phrase and say that the names for the Persons of the Trinity are but the "tip of the iceberg." But an iceberg floats and melts! A stronger image for the names of the Trinity might be an island. It might appear that an island is floating in the vast sea, but actually every island is the tip of a mountain, rooted deep in the fathomless abyss of the ocean. Even more rooted in the fathomless are our names for God, including those names for the Trinity: they are merely the island that we see sticking out of the sea.

What we'd like to do now is explore the rest of the mountain that sustains those islands and move beyond the God of our imagination, the God of our projections and desires. This exercise hopefully will give us a greater appreciation for the depth of the meaning of the Persons of the Trinity as we have known them in our limited way until now.

May the words of this prayer poem of St. Catherine of Siena be our guide:

You, eternal Trinity, you are a sea:
The more I enter you, the more I discover,
and the more I discover, the more I seek you. . . .

O abyss! O eternal Godhead! O deep sea!
What more could you have given me than the gift
     of your very self?
You are a fire always burning but never consuming;
you are a fire consuming in your heat all the soul's selfish
     love;
you are a fire lifting all chill and giving light.
In your light you have made me know your truth.[3]

---

[3]Catherine of Siena, *The Dialogue*, #167, trans. Suzanne Noffke, OP (New York: Paulist Press, 1980), 364–365. Sense lines mine.

1

Beginning and End

PERSONHOOD, TRINITY, AND RELATIONSHIP WEBS

Along the way we are going to redefine or at least clarify some terms. We Christians speak of God as a "person." This already raises alarm bells for people who are suspicious of "ole time religion." We also go on to teach that there are actually *three* persons in God, a teaching that certainly confounds our monotheistic sisters and brothers. But do we really understand this concept ourselves?

What does "person" mean, particularly in reference to the Trinity? "Person" is actually a multivalent term, open to lots of interpretations and understandings. Yes, Jesus is God-Made-Flesh, for instance, but we must not think of "person" as being equivalent to "human being" because that doesn't apply to the First Person, despite the prevalence of images of God as an old man. Nor does it apply to the Third Person. In using the word "person" we are not primarily speaking about anything in human form. Therefore, we'll have to be a little iconoclastic and wipe our slate clean of human beings, males or females, for the moment—even our notions of Father and Son—and start all over again.

Raimundo Panikkar, the great Spanish Indian scholar priest,

noted that "neither the actual words nor the concepts of *nature* or *person* are ever used in the New Testament to express the mystery of the Trinity." So he points out that the first generation of Christians "lived out their faith without ever using the words 'person' or 'nature.' "[1] These words were added to the Christian vocabulary later, when Christians were trying to make sense of and articulate their faith using Greek philosophical terms.

Second, Panikkar said that "person is neither singular nor plural."

> The person is not just a quantifiable reality, and the person has no meaning in the singular. An "I" implies a "thou"—and a he and a she and an it and a we and an us and all together; otherwise it's not a person. And, it has no plural because an I and a thou is not many; it's just part of the dimensions of the personal being.[2]

Another way he explained it is by pointing out the difference between a person and an individual. An *individual* is an abstraction, a manageable entity with clear-cut boundaries, an identifiable piece standing on its own, isolated: "It responds to an 'identification card' and has a social security number."

> The person, on the other hand, encompasses the whole complex web of the constitutive relationships . . . with no limits other than those which spontaneously appear in each case. An I is a *person* only to the extent that it does not isolate itself: a *thou* is needed, precisely in order to be an I. And vice versa. An individual is a closed system. Its boundaries are clear-cut. The mine and the thine cannot be mixed. A person is an open system.[3]

[1]Raimundo Panikkar, *The Trinity and the Religious Experience of Man* (Maryknoll, NY: Orbis Books, 1973), 41.

[2]"Of Lasting Value: Raimon Panikkar, Bruno Barnhart, and Donald Nicholl in Conversation about Eucharist," *Journal of Ecumenical Studies* 51, no. 1 (Winter 2016): 131.

[3]Raimundo Panikkar, *Blessed Simplicity: The Monk as Universal Archetype* (New York: Seabury, 1982), 71.

Pierre Teilhard de Chardin agrees:

> To be fully ourselves it is in the direction of convergence with all the rest, that we must advance—toward the "other." The goal of ourselves, the acme of our originality, is not our individuality but our *person*: and according to the evolutionary structure of the world, we can only find our person by uniting together.[4]

And according to Evelyn Underhill, this is one of the characteristics of the mystic, "the abolition of individuality: the hard separateness," the "I, Me, Mine" which makes of the person an isolated thing.[5] Richard Rohr agrees too and ties it in with the Trinity saying that if the Trinity reveals that God is relationship itself, then the goal of the spiritual journey is to discover and move toward connectedness on ever new levels. "Without connectedness and communion, we don't exist fully as our truest selves. Becoming who we really are is a matter of learning how to become more and more deeply connected."[6]

This is an important, consequential point: just as a person is an open system, so too the web of relationships that is the Trinity is not a closed system. Here is a hint of the fourth pole.

PANIKKAR'S APPROACH TO THE TRINITY

Panikkar introduced an understanding of the Trinity that has been tremendously influential for me, particularly in my work in interreligious dialogue. I break his teaching down into four points. He says that the Trinity has a universality that enables us to see the great spiritual traditions as dimensions of each other.

---

[4] Pierre Teilhard de Chardin, *Phenomenon of Man* (New York: Harper Colophon, 1975), 263.

[5] Evelyn Underhill, *Mysticism* (New York: Meridian Books, 1955), 71.

[6] Richard Rohr, *Near Occasions of Grace* (Maryknoll, NY: Orbis Books, 1993), 51.

First of all, *the Persons of the Trinity reflect essential aspects of the religious experience itself,* a universality, and so the Trinity is found as a pattern throughout all the world's religions and philosophies. He then describes three aspects of the divinity and three forms of spirituality that correspond to those three aspects: the First Person relates to the silent apophatic dimension of spirituality; the Second Person relates to the personalist dimension; and the Spirit, the Third Person, to the immanent dimension. In another place he puts it this way—and this may be definitive since it is from his last major work, *The Rhythm of Being*:

> Our symbols are the Father, the Son, and the Spirit, or in other words, Emptiness, Knowledge, and Love; although we could equally say, mysticism, intellectuality, and action.[7]

Father	Emptiness	mysticism
Son	Knowledge	intellectuality
Spirit	Love	action

I find this powerful, affecting, and highly significant for what comes next.

Second, *every authentic spiritual tradition particularly reflects one of these aspects.* If the First Person (deftly avoiding the name "Father" for the time being) represents the silence, then, for example, Buddhism can be seen as a "religion of the Father" or a religion of the First Person. The Second Person could be approached two different ways: either the personalist dimension of the devotional traditions, or God as an "interventionist" in the prophetic traditions—Word-Logos-Wisdom of Jews and Christians as well as Muslims, who call the three prophetic traditions *ahl al- Kitab*—the People of the Book—but also the *logos* traditions of philosophy East and West, particularly Taoism about which we will say much more below.

---

[7]Raimon Panikkar, *Rhythm of Being: The Unbroken Trinity* (Maryknoll, NY: Orbis Books, 2010), 323.

The Third Person, Panikkar says, represents the immanent dimension of the universal spiritual quest, indwelling, and so, according to him a representative would be *Advaita Vedanta* of India. But I will argue instead, and I think my confrere Bruno would agree with me, that the Third Person even more represents energy, and so the wisdom of the earth-based traditions, the primal peoples and tribal traditions and even *kundalini* and *chi* of the Asian traditions. That's Bruno's Music. (I'll explain this later.)

Third, following on that, according to Panikkar, the Christian notion of the Trinity can provide a kind of overarching pattern for seeing these universal spiritual attitudes, which are fundamental to humankind as they have been identified in the major religions of the world, *in relationship to each other when we see them operating together in the Persons of the Trinity.*

> The Trinity, then, may be considered as a junction where the authentic spiritual dimensions of all religions meet. . . . In the Trinity a true encounter of religions takes place, which results, not in a vague fusion or mutual dilution, but in an authentic enhancement of all the religious and even cultural elements that are contained in each.[8]

Finally, it could be that Christians may not even know or understand the depth of the mystery of the Trinity—nor find the fullness of those energies in ourselves—until we have opened to and responded in depth to the Trinitarian dimensions as found in these other traditions.

I, for example, didn't learn about silence and the apophatic dimension of the spiritual life in Catholic grade school, high school, or college, nor anywhere in my first thirty-two years of being a Catholic. I learned it from Buddhism and from Advaita

---

[8]Panikkar, *The Trinity and the Religious Experience of Man*, 42. It continues, "The Trinity is God's self-revelation in the fullness of time, the consummation both of all that God has already said of himself to [us] and of all that [we have] been able to know of God in [our] thought and mystical experience."

Vedanta of Hinduism, and only then found it in my own tradition. I certainly got a lot of *logos* theology all the way through, but new depths opened for me through the humanities, also through studying other world religions' philosophical underpinnings. What has become just as important to me is the dynamism of the Spirit of God that I have learned from kundalini yoga, or the Chinese tradition of *chi*, and from the animist way of seeing the universe common to the native peoples of America.

NEXT: FINDING THE TRINITY IN OURSELVES

What other ways to name the Persons of the Trinity might there be? In addition to the revered and scriptural *Father, Son, and Spirit,* we often hear *Creator, Redeemer, and Spirit* being used as alternates. But we are always in danger when we reduce the Persons of the Trinity to their functions.

There is, as Panikkar wrote, the beautiful expression *Emptiness, Knowledge, and Love.* Another way to name the Trinity, beloved in India, is *Sat-Chit-Ananda*: Being, Knowledge, and Bliss. This is a Hindu descriptor for God particularly dear to me and my fellow Camaldolese due to our ashram in South India—Saccidananda Ashram or the Ashram of the Holy Trinity. The founders of that ashram, Jules Monchanin, Abhishktananda (Henri le Saux), and Bede Griffiths, all saw this Hindu intuition as an intimation of the Trinity as well, the First Person as Being, the Second as Knowledge or Consciousness, and the Third as Bliss. Another of Panikkar's poetic trinities is *mysticism, intellectuality, and action.* And then there is Bruno's *Silence, Word, and Music.*

Here is a beautiful meditation from the fourteenth-century German Dominican spiritual teacher John Tauler from his *Spiritual Conferences* that can serve to bring this home. He teaches that there are many wonderful things that could be said on this subject of the Trinity, "and yet it is impossible to convey any adequate idea of how the essential and transcendent unity can issue in distinctions." At any rate:

It is much better to have experience of the Trinity than to talk about it. We should learn to find the Trinity in ourselves, and realize how we are in a real way formed according to its image. If we want to experience this we must turn inward, away from the activities of our faculties, both exterior and interior, away from all imaginations and all the notions we have acquired from outside ourselves, and sink and lose ourselves in the depths. Then the power of the Father will come and call the soul into himself through his only-begotten Son, and as the Son is born of the Father and returns to the Father, so we are born of the Father in the Son and flow back into the Father through the Son, becoming one with him. When this happens, the Holy Spirit pours himself out in unspeakable and overflowing love and joy, flooding and saturating the depths of our soul with his precious gifts.[9]

From this again we might glimpse the fourth element—finding the Trinity in *ourselves,* participating in the Trinity: "It is much better to have experience of the Trinity than to talk about it."

To bring all this to some greater clarity, let's reiterate Tauler using some of the other terms used to name the universal aspects of the spiritual life that the Persons of the Trinity represent. It is much better to have experience of the Trinity than to talk about it, find the Trinity in ourselves, and realize how we are in a real way formed according to its image. "If we want to experience this we must turn inward, away from the activities of our faculties, both exterior and interior, away from all imaginations and all the notions we have acquired from outside ourselves, and sink and lose ourselves in the depths." Then, using Bruno's terms, we could say,

> . . . the power of *Silence* will come
> and call the soul into Itself through *the Word,*
> and as *the Word* is born of the *Silence*

---

[9]From the "Spiritual Conferences," in *The Word in Season: Readings for the Liturgy of the Hours,* vol. 3, Trinity Sunday (Villanova, PA: Augustinian Press, 2001), 132.

and returns to *Silence,*
so we are born of *Silence* in *the Word*
and flow back into *Silence* through *the Word,*
becoming one with *the Word.*
When this happens, *the Music* pours itself out
in unspeakable and overflowing love and joy,
flooding and saturating the depths of our soul
     with precious gifts.

Or—if we turn inward, away from the activities of our faculties,
and sink and lose ourselves in the depths—

the power of *Emptiness* will come
and call the soul into Itself through *Knowledge,*
and as *Knowledge* is born of the *Emptiness*
and returns to *Emptiness,*
so we are born of *Emptiness* in *Knowledge*
and flow back to *Emptiness* through *Knowledge,*
becoming one with *Knowledge.*
When this happens, *Love* pours itself out
in unspeakable and overflowing love and joy,
flooding and saturating the depths of our soul
     with precious gifts.

Or we could say . . .

Then the power of *Being* will come
and call the soul into Itself through *Consciousness,*
and as *Consciousness* is born of *Being*
and returns to *Being,*
so we are born of *Being* in *Consciousness*
and flow back into *Being* through *Consciousness,*
becoming one with *Consciousness.*
When this happens, *Bliss* pours itself out
in unspeakable and overflowing love and joy,

flooding and saturating the depths of our soul
with precious gifts.

THE DANCE OF PERICHORESIS

It has become commonplace and popular to talk about the
"dance of the Trinity." It is also very fitting and in keeping with
what it means to be a person because a person is neither singular
nor plural: an I needs a thou and a thou needs an I, and a we and
an us and an all together, a whole web of relationships. The Greek
word the ancients came up with to describe this relationship was
perichoresis—*peri*–meaning "around" and *choresis*–"to give way."
Each Person in the Trinity gives way to the others, just as each of
these energies is always involved with the others.[10]

The good news is, and here we stumble onto the fourth element
again, *there is room in the dance for us too!* The Trinity gives way to
us too. Panikkar moved from using the word "theandric" meaning, God and humanity, to "cosmotheandric"—God, the human
person, and the cosmos. These three are always entwined, and he
uses the same word for this relationship that the ancients used for
the Trinity: *perichoresis.* This too is a perichoresis, a giving way.

> The World, Human and God are intimately woven in a
> *perichóresis.* A world without human beings makes no sense,
> a God without creatures would cease to be God. Human
> without World could no longer subsist and without God
> would not be truly human.[11]

---

[10] *Perichoresis* is *not*, by the way, related to the word "choreography" which actually
comes from the Greek word *khoros* as in a "chorus," though that would have been nice.

[11] Raimundo Panikkar, *Il silenzio del Buddha: Un ateismo religioso* (Milan: Mondadori, 2006), 170–171. The English version of this tames the sentence somewhat
by leaving out the term perichoresis: "The world, humankind, and God are as it were
incompatible as three separate, independent entities. They are intertwined." *The Silence
of God: The Answer of the Buddha,* trans. from the Italian by Robert Barr (Maryknoll,
NY: Orbis Books, 1990), 97. The statement, that "God without creatures would cease

None of the words that philosophy normally uses to describe the relationship between God and creation, between Absolute Reality and everything else, between the One and the many, were adequate for Panikkar, monism or dualism or pantheism or atheism or theism—or even monotheism. Only *perichoresis*, mutually giving way in this great Dance. If we focus on quantity—the number three—instead of the unity, we are thinking wrong. Panikkar often quoted St. Augustine in this regard, "Those who begin to number in the Trinity begin to err."[12]

The same thing we said about numbers in the Trinity applies to monotheism. This is an insight that is especially valuable in the conversation with Judaism and Islam, both of which are completely baffled by our belief in the Trinity! (It also may be that we don't really understand it ourselves.)

The term "monotheism" wasn't actually coined until the seventeenth century, so our understanding of what the oneness of God means is actually modern. In our scientific age, inadvertently perhaps, we think of "one" as a number, and so God is thought to be some kind of a solitary entity who stands apart from everything else, standing apart from all other creatures as well as all other gods, and therefore God can be seen as antagonistic to everything else as well. If we understand "oneness" in that way, then God can easily be a source of conflict and competition, our god against all the other gods, as if God had some kind of ego to defend or territory to protect.

But the Oneness of God shouldn't be understood mathematically or scientifically or even philosophically. The Oneness of God has to be understood *spiritually*, meaning not to think of "oneness" as a matter of *quantity*. God's oneness is a *quality* not a quantity. What the Oneness of God is affirming is a unity. God's Oneness

---

to be God," could be easily misconstrued. It ought to be understood in the same way that Meister Eckhart says, "God becomes God when all other creatures speak God forth." In other words, as William Harmless masterfully explains, "When God created the world, when he spoke the world into being, the world in turn spoke back. . . . God thus became 'God' only when something other than God came into being." William Harmless, SJ, *Mystics* (New York: Oxford University Press, 2008), 118.

[12]"Of Lasting Value," 133.

does not mean a being who stands apart from creation. More than God's Oneness meaning an entity who is radically different and superior to creation, it means the One who always is present to creation, as the reconciliation of all oppositions.[13]

The Trinity is not a closed system! The fourth element that Bruno adds is the Trinity *and the Cosmos*, the Trinity *and Creation*, and he calls that the Dance, not just the Trinity dancing among themselves, but the Trinity dancing with the cosmos, a God totally beyond our grasp and yet strangely close and familiar. The Silence, the Word, the Music, and this Dance. If we could understand more about these complementary poles in us—the energy of the silence, the word, the music—we could unlock the unrealized potential of our Christian spirituality and join the dance. Because we too are a part of that Cosmos, a member of Creation, a partner in the Dance. Realizing our union with God and our union with creation go hand in hand. This we will explore in the pages ahead.

God manifests in history through Word and Spirit, the two who are revealed in the New Testament but who are already glimpsed in the Jewish scriptures, as we shall see. But following on that, "The One (God) is manifested to and participated in by created beings through the Word and Spirit." One of Bruno's favorite phrases was "participatory consciousness." I like to turn that around and also say "conscious participation." Participation in what? Divinity itself! This is our *telos*–our ultimate goal as Christians, participation in divinity. The Second Letter of Peter states that:

Thus God has given us, through these things, his precious and very great promises, so that through them you may escape from the corruption that is in the world because of lust, and may become participants of the divine nature.[14]

---

[13]James Carroll, *Jerusalem, Jerusalem: How the Ancient City Ignited Our Modern World* (Boston: Houghton Mifflin Harcourt, 2011), 61. Carroll quotes the twelfth-century Jewish sage Moses Maimonides: "The term 'one' is just as applicable to God as the term 'many.'"

[14]2 Pt. 1:4.

And this is what the priest says while pouring the water into the wine at the altar in the Roman Rite:

> By the mystery of this water and wine,
> *may we come to share the divinity of Christ*
> who humbled himself to share in our humanity.

I am delightfully surprised at how many times this theme of participation appears in the newest translations of the collects for the Mass in the Roman Rite. For the Solemnity of the Annunciation the first translation from the Latin after the Council prayed that just as "your Word became flesh . . . may we become more like Jesus." That's nice enough. Now it reads, more accurately, "O God, who willed that your Word should take on the reality of human flesh in the womb of the Virgin Mary," grant that we may "become partakers even in his divine nature," echoing the prayer of the water being poured into the wine.

God–Word–Spirit–created beings: this is "not a closed system."

As noted, Panikkar returns to the theme of "person" often. One of the most concrete poetic versions of it is in *Christophany*, in which he writes that we may "describe the person as a knot in a web of relations." Note here again the difference between an individual and a person:

> In such a perspective individuality is no more than the knot cut away from all the threads that contribute to make it up. The knot without the thread is nothing, and the threads without the knot could not subsist. . . . A knot is a knot because it is made up of threads tied together with other knots by means of a network of threads. Although the knots are not unreal, neither are the threads. The network constitutes one great whole.[15]

---

[15]Raimon Panikkar, *Christophany: The Fullness of Man,* trans. Alfred DiLascia (Maryknoll, NY: Orbis Books, 2004), 61.

None of it is unreal, but neither does anything exist without the other.

That reminds us of the well-known poetic words of Chief Seattle. The first part is quoted often: "The earth does not belong to us; we belong to the earth." But what follows on that is even more sublime:

All things are connected like the blood that unites us all.
We did not weave the web of life; we are merely a strand
   in it.
Whatever we do to the web, we do to ourselves.

A PLACE AT THE TABLE

There are two icons in our chapel at New Camaldoli Hermitage that reveal to me what the fourth element is in Christianity. I'll speak of one of those icons now and the other at the very end.

Whenever I give a tour of our chapel, I always bring guests in through the front entrance and spend time there telling this whole story, because there we have a rendering of the famous icon of the great fourteenth- to fifteenth-century Russian iconographer Andrei Rublev, a work called either simply *The Trinity* or *The Hospitality of Abraham*. This icon is also a great symbol of this fourth pole or movement. It's based on the enigmatic story from Genesis 18, when "the Lord" appears to Abraham under the terebinths of Mamre (modern-day Hebron) as "three beings" or "three angels." As Rublev assumes in his icon so we too assume that these three are an intimation of the Trinity.

There are many things that could be and have been said about this icon, including the significance of all the colors. But the element that serves our purpose here is more about its seating arrangement and choreography. The hand of the figure on our right, representing the Spirit, points toward an open fourth place at the table. At the front of the table there appears to be a little rectangular hole. There is residue of what possibly could be glue on that spot on the original icon, and some art historians think that at one time there was a mirror glued to the front of the table. There was room at this table for a fourth guest—the observer, the one in the mirror, you, me. Not only does that mirror seem to have been lost over the centuries, more importantly our understanding of who God is and who we are in relationship to God seems to have been lost too. There's a place at the table—for me, for us, and for all creation.

This is the reason I like it at the entrance to our chapel: at least intuitively, when people come in I want them to have a sense of invitation, openness, welcome, hospitality; and even more to feel as if they are walking into the love life and the choreography of the Trinity. And that is the fourth element: walking into the love life of the Trinity, joining in the Dance, the perichoresis of the cosmo-the-andric: God, creation and the human always intertwined.

There is a wonderful passage from an anonymous Carthusian in the book *The Wound of Love.* He writes, "But you will permit me the risk of saying that for all of us God must die at a certain moment. In one sense only the atheist can truly believe in God." And then he hurries to explain:

It is necessary that the God of our imagination die, the God of our projections and desires (who is none other than our Ego deified); the God who stands alongside the cosmos as some-"thing" else, who stands alongside the neighbor as someone else, in competition with him or her to win my love; the God of whom it suffices to know the general moral rules in order to do his will; the God infinitely above his creatures' pains in a transcendence beyond reach; the God-judge, who punishes in accord with a justice conceived along human lines; the God who blocks the spontaneity of life and love. Such a God must die to make room for a God strangely close and familiar and nevertheless totally beyond our grasp [I would turn that around and also say "a God totally beyond our grasp and yet strangely close and familiar"!]; a God who bears a human face, that of Christ, that of my brother; who is love in a way that defies all our human notions of justice; who is generosity, overflowing life, gratuitousness, unpredictable liberty.[16]

With all this in mind, I ask you, as we continue this journey, to turn inward, away from the activities of our faculties, both exterior and interior, away from all imaginations and all the notions we have acquired from outside ourselves, and sink and lose ourselves in the depths. Let's meet the Divine again, from the ground up, one Person at a time, but always in relation with all the rest.

---

[16] *The Wound of Love: A Carthusian Miscellany*, Anon. (Kalamazoo, MI: Cistercian Publications, 1994), 123–124.

2

The Silence

I will rearticulate our understanding of the First Person of the Trinity in three different ways, which will build one on the other: the First Person as the silent apophatic depth, then as the font of Being, and finally as the Great Mother. I will still for the most part try to avoid the word, the name, and the title "Father." This is not to diminish God as Father in any way, as Jesus introduces God to us, but just the opposite. I find myself appreciating God the Father more, and more broadly, once I uncover the rest of the mystery of this first person.

I remember attending a liturgical conference at which the late great theologian Cardinal Avery Dulles gave a wonderful speech. In the question-and-answer period that followed, someone challenged him asking, "Isn't 'Father' only a metaphor?" To which he responded, in his grand stentorian voice, "Yes, but it's an *inspired* metaphor." Referring to God as *Abba* is central to Jesus' experience, but a very unusual way for a Jew to refer to God. Even "father" is not used that often in scripture before Jesus. At the same time, though we assume this would have been Jesus' word in Aramaic, the actual term *Abba* is used only once in the gospels, in the Gospel of Mark during the agony in the garden, and twice mentioned by Paul.[1]

---

[1] Mk. 14:36; Rom. 8:15; Gal. 4:6.

Both Bruno and Panikkar suggest that the First Person dimension is the Silence which in Christianity is represented by the Father. We are going to expand even beyond the Silence of the First Person, but this is where we start, with what we call the "apophatic depth" of God, the fathomless abyss of the godhead, the God beyond all name and form of the mystical traditions.

THE APOPHATIC

Some years ago my nephew had an injury to the head from a work accident and for a few weeks afterward he was what the doctors called "aphasic." That word comes from the Greek *a-* ("not") and *phanai* ("speak")—not speaking. In other words, he could not communicate with words. The word "apophatic" comes from the Greek prefix *apo-* meaning "away from" and the same root, *phanai*, "to speak" and is related to the Greek word *apophatikos* which means negative, and *apophasis*, "denial." Hence, apophatic theology teaches that knowledge of God is obtained through negation. This as contrasted with most of our theology which is *kata-phatic*, according to communication or speech. This apophatic approach is also referred to classically as the *via negativa*, the "negative way" to God. As Pope Benedict describes it, this type of theology and spirituality is "marked by the conviction that it is impossible to say who God is," and that only negative expressions can be used to speak of God, "that God can only be spoken of with 'no,' and that it is only possible to reach him by entering into this experience of 'no.' "[2]

Bruno and Panikkar relate this silent apophatic dimension to the First Person of the Trinity since it could be argued that in the Christian scriptures the Father expressed himself only through the Son, and of himself has no word or expression. In the gospels, Jesus speaks; the Father says only, "Listen to him!" (Mt. 17:5; Mk. 9:7;

---

[2]Pope Benedict XVI, *Great Christian Thinkers: From the Early Church through the Middle Ages* (Minneapolis: Fortress Press, 2011), 132–133.

Lk. 9:35). It's different in the more mythological Hebrew scriptures, but we shall look into that a bit as well.

That being said, the spirituality of the First Person in this pure apophatic form still rarely appears in Christianity as it does in Buddhism, for instance, rarely even in scripture, at least not explicitly. The idea of the "silence of the Father" does appear in the patristic era, however, for example Ignatius of Antioch, who wrote, "There is only one God, revealed by Jesus Christ his Son, who is his Word sprung from the silence."[3] John of the Cross echoes this centuries later when he writes that "the Father spoke one Word, which was his Son, and this Word he always speaks in eternal silence, and in silence must it be heard by the soul."

One scriptural passage that is used often in the Christmas season is from the Book of Wisdom. It's the entrance antiphon in the Roman Missal for the Sixth Day within the Octave of Christmas.

> For while gentle silence enveloped all things,
>   and night in its swift course was now half gone,
>   your all-powerful word leaped from heaven,
>   from the royal throne. (Wis. 18:14–15)

Robert Cardinal Sarah reflected in his book *The Power of Silence* that "this verse would be understood by the Christian liturgical tradition as a prefiguration of the silent Incarnation of the Word."[4] Long before him, the eleventh- to twelfth-century Cistercian abbot Blessed Guerric of Igny commented on that same passage saying, "Your almighty Word, O Lord, which made its way down in deep silence from the Father's royal throne into the cattle stall, speaks to us better for its silence. Let anyone who has ears to hear listen to what

---

[3]Ignatius of Antioch, *Letter to the Magnesians*, 8, 2 (SC 10, 102), quoted in Olivier Clement, *The Roots of Christian Mysticism: Texts from the Patristic Era with Commentary*, 2nd ed. (Hyde Park, NY: New City Press, 1993), 36.

[4]Robert Sarah, *The Power of Silence: Against the Dictatorship of Noise* (San Francisco: Ignatius Press, 2017), 24.

this holy and loving silence of the eternal Word is saying to us."[5]

Here is the "silence of the Father": the Second Person of the Trinity is born of the silence of the First Person.

HINTS IN JEWISH SCRIPTURE

Besides Wisdom 18, a few other texts from the Jewish scriptures come to mind. One is from the beautiful Isaiah canticle:

> Truly, you are a God who hides himself,
> O God of Israel, the Savior.
> All of them are put to shame and confounded,
> the makers of idols go in confusion together.
>   (Is. 45:15–16)

Remember the admonitions against any graven images that are so foundational to the covenant with Moses. When Exodus 20 forbids images (repeated in Deuteronomy and Leviticus), it mainly seems to be in reference to having no other gods in the form of idols:

> I am the Lord your God,
> who brought you out of the land of Egypt,
> out of the house of slavery;
> you shall have no other gods before me.
> You shall not make for yourself an idol,
> whether in the form of anything that is in heaven above,
> or that is on the earth beneath, or that is in the water
>   under the earth.
> You shall not bow down to them or worship them.
>   (Ex. 20:2–5)

---

[5] *Sermo 5 in ativitate Domini* 1–2 (SC 166, 223–226); in *Christ Our Light: Patristic Readings on Gospel Themes*, trans. and ed. Friends of Henry Ashworth, Second Sunday after Christmas (Riverdale, MD: Exordium Books, 1981), 68.

But in another place in the Book of Deuteronomy the admonition against idols seems to have an apophatic context:

> *Since you saw no form when the Lord spoke to you at Horeb*
>   *out of the fire,*
> take care and watch yourselves closely,
> so that you do not act corruptly by making an idol for
>   yourselves,
> in the form of any figure—the likeness of male or female.
>   (Dt. 4:15)

"You" here is referring to Moses, and Horeb is referring to Exodus 3, when God appears to Moses in the burning bush. So, since I, the Lord, did not appear to you in a form, not only should there be no idols of other gods, but there shall be no image of God at all.

There were certainly no images of God the Father at the beginning of the Christian era, and you can imagine the perplexity of Jewish people when iconography of God the Father does start to appear in the Christian dispensation. As a matter of fact, during the iconoclastic controversy of the eighth century, which we will discuss below, Emperor Leo thought that use of icons at all was the chief obstacle to the conversion of Jews and Muslims. The Catholic Catechism addresses it this way: "The divine injunction included the prohibition of every representation of God by human hands." Then it points to that same passage from Deuteronomy 4 saying, "It is the absolutely transcendent God who revealed himself to Israel."[6]

Where Catholicism gets around that, if you will, is by pointing out that "already in the Old Testament, God ordained or permitted the making of images that pointed symbolically toward salvation by the incarnate Word," that is, the Second Person of the Trinity—the bronze serpent in Numbers, the ark of the covenant and the cherubim in Exodus 25, among other places. The Catechism then

---

[6]*Catechism of the Catholic Church* (Città del Vaticano: Libreria Editrice Vaticana, 1994), #2129.

goes on to speak about the iconoclasts, and so on, and the proper use of images: "The honor paid to sacred images is a 'respectful veneration,' not the adoration due to God alone."[7]

Remember too that the Prophet Muhammad's first action when he conquered Mecca was to remove statues and images from the Ka'bah. He wanted to bring the Arabic people back to the pure covenant with Abraham and away from their polytheistic idolatry. (According to reports collected by Ibn Ishaq and al-Azraqi he did, however, spare a painting of Mary and Jesus, and a fresco of Abraham.) According to a *hadith*:

> When the Prophet entered Mecca on the day of the Conquest, there were 360 idols around the Ka'bah. The Prophet started striking them with a stick he had in his hand and was saying, "Truth has come and Falsehood has Vanished."[8]

THE SOUND OF SHEER SILENCE

Another hint of the apophatic we get from the Jewish scriptures is from the nineteenth chapter of the First Book of Kings, when God told Elijah to stand on the mountain before the Lord, for the Lord was about to pass by.

> Now there was a great wind, so strong that it was splitting mountains and breaking rocks in pieces before the Lord, but the Lord was not in the wind; and after the wind an earthquake, but the Lord was not in the earthquake; and after the earthquake a fire, but the Lord was not in the fire; and after the fire a sound of sheer silence. When Elijah heard it, he wrapped his face in his mantle and went out and stood at the entrance of the cave.

---

[7]Ibid., #2132.
[8]Sahih al-Bukhari, *Book 59, Hadith 583. Cf.* Qur'an 17:81.

Then there came a voice to him that said, "What are you doing here, Elijah?" He answered, "I have been very zealous for the Lord, the God of hosts." (1 Kgs. 19:9b–14a)

Just before this, Elijah has been running away from the wicked Queen Jezebel. But "his flight soon becomes a journey out of the ordinary world, symbolized by leaving behind companionship and food, and a pilgrimage to a sacred place."[9] There are various poetic translations of those culminating words, the "sound of sheer silence." Sometimes it is rendered "a whispering sound." It's very popular to refer to the "still small voice," as in the well-known English hymn: "Speak through the earthquake, wind and fire, / O still small voice of calm!" But "the sound of sheer silence" or a "fine silence" is most accurate.

That last line is all important: God asks, "What are you doing *here*?" Cardinal Sarah comments that one day, "beyond the invasive noise that is perversely interwoven in so many lives," it will be important to listen once again to that "still small voice," the voice that is going to ask *us*, "What are you doing *here*?"[10] There's a commission after the theophany; the commission comes only *after* the theophany, after the experience of God in silence; the understanding of the commission comes only in the silence where God is.

Notice also that this whole scene, including Elijah's veiling his face, recalls the theophany promised to Moses in Exodus 33 (and again in Exodus 34) when Moses implores God, "Show me your glory" and God says:

"I will make all my goodness pass before you, and will proclaim before you the name. . . . But," he said, "you cannot see my face; for no one shall see me and live." And the Lord

---

[9] *The New Jerome Biblical Commentary*, ed. Raymond Brown, Joseph Fitzmeyer, and Roland Murphy (Hoboken, NJ: Prentice Hall, 1990), 172.

[10] Sarah, *The Power of Silence*, 85.

continued, "See, there is a place by me where you shall stand on the rock; and while my glory passes by I will put you in a cleft of the rock, and I will cover you with my hand until I have passed by; then I will take away my hand, and you shall see my back; but my face shall not be seen." (33:17–23)

Rabbi Lawrence Kushner points out that the Hebrew word for "my back" (*achorai*) in this passage doesn't just have a spatial sense to it, but a temporal sense as well, and he says we miss the whole point if we read it literally and imagine that God has a backside.

What God seems to be saying to Moses is that you can see my "afterward." You can see what it's like just after I've been there. But if you knew what it was like when I was there, that would mean you were still hanging on to a little piece of your self-awareness that was telling you it was you who was there. And that would also mean there was a part of your consciousness detached and watching the whole thing, and therefore *not all of you* was there. There are, in other words, simply some things in life that demand such total self-absorption that you cannot even know that it's you there until it's over. Being in the presence of God is such an experience.[11]

Kushner also tells this story about Gershom Scholem, the mid-twentieth-century German-born Israeli philosopher and historian. His main contribution was a revivification of the Kabbalah tradition of Jewish mysticism. We learn in both Exodus and Numbers that "the Lord used to speak to Moses face to face, as one speaks to a friend: 'With him I speak face to face—clearly, not in riddles, and he beholds the form of the Lord'" (Ex. 33:11, Nm. 12:8). Rabbi Kushner explains that there is a mystical tradition that says that God didn't actually give the whole five books of Moses, that

---

[11]Lawrence Kushner, *Jewish Spirituality: A Brief Introduction for Christians* (Woodstock, VT: SkyLight Paths, 2001), 69.

God didn't even give the whole ten utterances. (The "ten utterances" sometimes, as here, refers to the Ten Commandments, and sometimes refers to the ten times in the Book of Genesis God says *Yehi*—"Let there be . . ." while creating the world. In the Kabbalah tradition they are seen as parallel.) There's another tradition that said that God gave just the first two commandments or utterances: "I am the LORD your God, who brought you out of the land of Egypt, out of the house of slavery. You shall have no other gods before me" (Ex. 20:2–3).

In his study of the Kabbalah, Gershom Scholem uncovered a Hasidic teacher named Mendel Torum of Rymanov who takes it even farther. He insisted that God didn't even give the first utterance on Sinai, nor even the first word, the Hebrew word *anochi*, the first person singular "I." Mendel Torum taught that God only gave the very first letter of the first word, the Hebrew letter *aleph*, which is generally considered to be soundless. Scholem, however, pointed out that that's not quite correct: the sound of *aleph* (which also has the numerical equivalent of the number 1) is actually the noise that the larynx makes as it clicks into gear. It's a barely audible little click. And that's what God gave at Mount Sinai, a barely audible little sound.

Mendel Torum of Rymanov's teaching makes the revelation a mystical one. Rabbi Kushner comments that,

> What happened at Mount Sinai was barely audible and had no particular sound; and it therefore became the job of, in this case, Moses the prophet, or of anyone else, to give human content to that otherwise unpronounceable sound. The Zohar says that the *aleph* is a seed in which is enwrapped the entire Torah, and what it means to be a religious person is to spend your life unpacking that seed.[12]

---

[12]Interview with Rabbi Kushner on the radio program "On Being," March 10, 2016; see also Kushner, *Jewish Spirituality,* 42.

I have often thought, with our regular practice of *lectio divina*, that what it means to be a monk is that very thing, to spend your life unpacking that seed. What it means to be a religious person is to spend your life giving human content to that still small voice. What it means to be a spiritual seeker is to spend our lives unwrapping what is enwrapped in that tiny, barely audible, click.

But what silence we must inhabit in order to first hear it! "In silence must it be heard by the soul."

GREGORY OF NYSSA AND PSEUDO-DIONYSIUS

In the Jewish scriptures the three passages in the Book of Exodus that Gregory of Nyssa comments on come to mind. Gregory was a fourth-century Cappadocian father, monk, and bishop. He was the younger brother of Basil the Great and is a saint as well. Gregory is considered the father of Christian mysticism and is the most influential early writer on the apophatic tradition. Gregory points to three of the encounters that Moses had with God in the Book of Exodus. In Exodus 3 Moses has an encounter with light in the burning bush. Later God speaks to him in a cloud: "Then Moses went up on the mountain, and the cloud covered the mountain. . . . Moses entered the cloud, and went up on the mountain . . . for forty days and forty nights" (24:15, 18). However, when he reached the top of Mount Sinai and was made perfect, he saw God in darkness: "Moses drew near to the thick darkness where God was" (Ex. 20:21). And this, Gregory says, shows us that the journey nearer to God as we increase in faith will be a gradual entrance into holy darkness of unknowing rather than an increase in light and knowledge.[13]

The thick darkness—*where God was.*

---

[13]Gregory of Nyssa, *Commentary on the Song* XI: 1000–1. In Andrew Louth, *The Origins of the Christian Mystical Tradition: From Plato to Denys* (Oxford: Clarendon Press, 1981), 83.

Now we are drawing near to the meaning of this holy darkness: the un-know-ability of God. We think we have got God all figured out with our formulae, kept in tidy little intellectual boxes and categories. But *si comprehendis, non est Deus*, Augustine said famously: "If you understand, then it's not God."[14] All of our theologizing is like "toy bears banging on cracked drums," in the words of poet Paul Claudel. Words are not algebraic formulae; words are always mere symbols. That's why it might be better to approach theology as if it were poetry rather than science. Some would argue that this was the dark side of Scholasticism, particularly when we get to the era of Neo-Scholasticism and Neo-Thomism in the late nineteenth century, which at its worst tried to formulize and intellectualize and objectify something that is essentially an experience and a relationship, an encounter. This is also why the language of mystics in every tradition is often held in suspicion; it does not fit into neat categories. How many songs have been written about falling in love, and do any of them capture all of it, or get it right once and for all?

The early Franciscan theologian Bonaventure, himself a great theologian, tells us to

> Seek the answer in God's grace, not in doctrine;
> in the longing of will, not in the understanding;
> in the sighs of prayer, not in research;
> seek the bridegroom, not the teacher;
> darkness, not daylight;
> and look not to the light but rather to the raging fire
> that carries the soul to God with intense fervor and glowing love.
> Let us die, then, and enter into the darkness,
> silencing our anxieties, our passions,
> and all the fantasies of our imagination.[15]

---

[14]*Sermo* 117, c. 3, 5 (PL 38:663).

[15]From the *Journey of the Mind to God*, by Saint Bonaventure (Cap. 7, 4. 6: *opera omnia* 5, 312–313), quoted in *The Office of Readings* (Boston: St. Paul Editions, 1983), 1474–1475.

Then there is Dionysius, or *Pseudo*-Dionysius, the Areopagite. He gets his name from a story in the Acts of the Apostles. While in Athens St. Paul was upset at seeing so many idols in the city. He spent time arguing with the Jews in the synagogue, and debating with Epicurean and Stoic philosophers in the marketplace. At one point they brought him to a place called the Areopagus, a hill above the city where trials concerning both homicides and religious matters were held. Paul's speech there is considered one of his most dramatic in Acts. He told them how among their objects of worship he had found an altar with the inscription "to an unknown god."

> What therefore you worship as unknown, this I proclaim to you. The God who made the world and everything in it, he who is Lord of heaven and earth, does not live in shrines made by human hands, nor is he served by human hands, as though he needed anything, since he himself gives to all mortals life and breath and all things. . . . For "In him we live and move and have our being"; as even some of your own poets have said, "For we too are his offspring." Since we are God's offspring, we ought not to think that the deity is like gold, or silver, or stone, an image formed by the art and imagination of mortals. (Acts 17:16–28)

Among those who joined Paul and became believers afterward were a woman named Damaris and a man named Dionysius.

The actual writer we are referring to is probably a fifth-century Syrian monk who takes the name, as was common practice in ancient times, hence known often as Pseudo-Dionysius the Areopagite. He wrote five major treatises, one of which is lost to us. His treatise *Divine Names* deals with positive or kataphatic theology, conceptual terms or names of God, attributes of God—God is good, holy, light, and so on. *Divine Names* also introduces the concept of negative or apophatic theology, that God is utterly unknowable, and no human language can express anything true about the divine. But where he really develops the concept of negative or apophatic theology is in a brief work called *Mystical Theology*. In it he writes:

> For the higher we soar in contemplation the more limited become our expressions of that which is purely intelligible; even as now, when plunging into the Darkness which is above the intellect, we pass not merely into brevity of speech, but even into absolute silence, of thoughts as well as words . . . until, the entire ascent being accomplished, we become wholly voiceless, inasmuch as we are absorbed in Him who is totally ineffable.[16]

His two remaining treatises, *Ecclesial Hierarchy* and *Celestial Hierarchies*, deal with how scripture and the liturgy can and should lead to the mystical. This is important, because there can be a tendency to think that we leave all that behind in the mystical way, instead of realizing that there is a constant conversation of symbols, ritual, and language that are meant to lead us to the mystical and that at their best are also manifestations and communications of the mystical. John Main, the late Benedictine teacher of Christian meditation, addressed this in his "Gethsemani Talks" regarding the fourteenth-century English contemplative writer Walter Hilton:

> Hilton is a good witness that there is no antipathy . . . between contemplative prayer, vocal prayer and liturgical prayer. He does trace a kind of progressive *development* through these forms but not in the sense that we ever get to a stage in our life when we have gone beyond liturgical prayer or vocal prayer. The development that he really sees is a growth in the delight with which one enters whatever form is appropriate at any time. And all these forms of prayer are, of course, complementary.[17]

---

[16]Dionysius the Areopagite, *The Mystical Theology and the Celestial Hierarchies*, trans. Editors of the Shrine of Wisdom (Surrey, UK: Shrine of Wisdom, 1965), 14.

[17]Quoted in John Main, *Silence and Stillness in Every Season: Daily Readings with John Main*, ed. Paul Harris (New York: Continuum, 2002), 91.

Why Pseudo-Dionysius, and why now? Pope Benedict XVI taught that in our times Pseudo-Dionysius has a new relevance. Just as he was a mediator between the Neo-Platonic Greek spirit and the Gospel, now he can serve "as a great mediator in the modern dialogue between Christianity and the mystical theologies of Asia" (we can assume he is referring here to Hinduism, Buddhism, and Taoism) all of which are ultimately marked by the same conviction we noted earlier in regard to the *via negativa*, that only negative expressions can be used to speak of God: "that God can only be spoken of with 'no,' and that it is only possible to reach him by entering into this experience of 'no.'" Here, the Emeritus Pope writes, is seen a similarity between the thought of the Areopagite and that of the Asian religions.[18]

THE "NO" EXPERIENCE OF GOD

This apophatic spirituality, this silence of the First Person, is similar to the Buddhist experience of nirvana, and also to the silence of the Taoist, and to a particular strain of thought in Hinduism known as *advaita Vedanta* (nonduality), found in the Upanishads, and *jnana-yoga* (the yoga of knowledge). The classic Sanskrit expression, found in the Brihadaranyaka Upanishad, is *neti neti*, which means "not this, not this," or "neither this, nor that."[19]

This Self is That which has been described as
neti neti—"Not this, Not this."
It is imperceptible, for It is never perceived;
undecaying, for It never decays;
unattached, for It is never attached;
unfettered—It never feels pain, and never suffers injury.[20]

---

[18]Pope Benedict XVI, *Great Christian Thinkers*, 132–133.
[19]Also in Chandogya Upanishad and in another text called the Avadhuta Gita. All quotations from Asian texts will be my own conflations drawn from various translations.
[20]Brihadaranaka Upanishad, IV-ii-4.

This helps us understand the nature of *Brahman*, the Ground of Being, by first understanding what is *not Brahman*. The "*neti neti* search" wants to negate all rationalizations and anything else that might distract us from a meditative awareness of reality beyond all concepts; this is one of the key elements of *jnana yoga*. We are also now on the threshold of Buddhism, even chronologically, since the birth of Buddhism coincides with the end of the Vedic era, *advaita Vedanta*, and the Upanishads in India. The Buddha's way is based totally on moving to the experience of apophatic silence by negating the way of logic, by swimming upstream, as it were, against the tide of thought, of *logos*.

This is the *scopos*-goal of the silent meditation practices that come to us from the Asian traditions, to which so many Western Jews and Christians have been drawn, just sitting (*shikantaza*) or concentration on a *koan* in the Zen traditions, focus on the breath, the use of a mantra, and so on. Christianity has rediscovered its own similar practice, as teachers such as John Main and Thomas Keating point us back to the pure prayer of the desert monks. This is a method of prayer and meditation which aims toward a one-pointed concentration rather than expanding thought through imagination or discursive thought. In this many Jews and Christians have found helpful techniques from the Asian traditions.

Panikkar says specifically Buddhism could be considered "the religion of the Father" since it is a tradition rooted in silence. I would add, especially in speaking of Taoism, it could also be considered a religion of the Great Mother, as we shall see below. The classic primary Taoist text, the Tao te Ching, begins with:

> The Tao that can be told is not the immortal Tao.
> The name that can be named is not the immortal name.
> The origin of heaven and earth has no name.
> Named it is the mother of the ten thousand things.

So, what do Taoism and Buddhism or *Advaita Vedanta* teach us about this Silence? About who and what we call the Father, the First

Person of the Trinity, this first universal movement of the spiritual journey? In this Asian experience of the silence a Christian might catch a glimpse, a reflection of the depths of the fathomless abyss of the godhead. For example, the Indian philosopher and yogi Sri Aurobindo in *Philosophy of the Upanishads* uses words that could easily apply to the Christian apophatic tradition. In the Upanishads it is distinctly stated that neither mind nor senses can reach God, indeed "words return baffled" from the attempt to describe God. So, he says:

> we do not discern the Absolute and transcendent in Its
>   reality,
> nor can we discriminate the right way
> or perhaps any way of teaching the reality of it to others;
> and it is even held that It can only be properly character-
>   ized in negative language
> and that to every challenge for definition
> the only true answer is NETI NETI, *It is not this, not that.*
> Brahman is not definable, not describable, not intellectu-
>   ally knowable. And yet . . .
> the Upanishads constantly declare that Brahman is the one
>   true object of knowledge
> and the whole of Scripture is in fact an attempt, not per-
>   haps to define,
> but at least in some sort to characterize and present an
>   idea,
> and even a detailed idea of Brahman.[21]

John Main puts it in a simple straightforward way: "You have to learn to let go of your ideas, to let go of the insights you have about yourself, or about God, or about meditation."[22] And Abhi-

---

[21]Sri Aurobindo, *The Philosophy of the Upanishads* (Pondicherry: Sri Aurobindo Ashram Press, 1994), 18–19. Sense lines mine.

[22]From *Door to Silence*, quoted in John Main, *Silence and Stillness in Every Season*, 84.

shiktananda, another profound Christian mystic, writes in his most famous book, *Prayer*, "Those whose aim is God never stop short at anything whatever is thought or felt, no matter how exalted or uplifting it may seem to be. God is beyond."[23]

In Western Christianity we have the mysticism of *The Cloud of Unknowing*, Meister Eckhart, and St. John of the Cross. However, a spirituality of the silence of the First Person rarely appears in this pure apophatic form for us as it does in Buddhism, Hinduism, or Taoism, especially in our scriptures.[24] If Christians could realize that the spiritual experience of Buddhists, Hindus, and Taoists are reflecting dimensions of their own Trinitarian spirituality, what an eye-opening experience it could be. Those traditions might help us at least catch a glimpse of this dimension in our own, especially if we let the Word lead us back to the Silence from which it came. (That is the title of John Main's best-known book on Christian meditation, *Word into Silence*.)

IN THE ANTECHAMBER OF GOD'S NAME

Bruno would add another aspect: What might *modern poetry* teach us about this first energy, this aspect of religious experience? As Wallace Stevens wrote in his *Adagia*, "The poet is the priest of the invisible." Even further, Stevens wrote that even if "one has abandoned a belief in god, poetry is that essence which takes

---

[23]Abhishiktananda, *Prayer: Exploring Contemplative Prayer through Eastern and Western Spirituality* (Delhi: ISPCK, 2015), 67.

[24]Ewert Cousins nuances it this way: "In Christianity, the Father and the Spirit are united through the Word. The Father's silence comes to expression in the generation of the Word; and the Spirit leads Christians to a differentiated and dialogic union with the Son, and through the Son to the Father. And so for Christians, the Word colors the spirituality of the Father and the Spirit, and integrates it. Our spirituality of the Father and our spirituality of the Spirit, our experience of the Father and the Spirit, our understanding of both the Father and Spirit, are always mediated by the Word. In other words, we always experience the Divine through, with and in the Word—we even experience the Silence in the Word." *Christ of the Twenty-first Century* (New York: Continuum, 1998), 82.

its place as life's redemption." We could see poetry as apophatic language when other religious language has lost its zest or become too commonplace and loaded with banalities and platitudes. Another prime and perhaps better example is Rainer Maria Rilke, particularly his *Book of Hours*, which reads like sacred scripture. Rilke was heavily influenced by Eastern Christianity, specifically the Russian Orthodox tradition, where the apophatic dimension tends to be a lot closer to the surface. As he wrote:

> Russia . . . opened itself to me and granted me the brotherliness and the darkness of God, in whom alone there is community. That was what I named him then, the God who had broken in upon me, and for a long time I lived in the antechamber of his name, on my knees. Now, you hardly ever hear me name him; there is an indescribable discretion between us, and where nearness and penetration once were, now distances stretch forth. . . . The comprehensible slips away, is transformed; instead of possession one learns relationship, and arises a namelessness that must begin once more in our relations with God if we are to be complete and without evasion.[25]

This could apply to the other arts as well, which are always striving for new ways of communicating, even in sound and image. Take for example the music of the great French composer Olivier Messiaen, the faithful traditional Catholic organist of the church of Saint Sulpice in Paris whose shockingly dissonant music does not sound like anything most ordinary listeners would recognize as typically sacred.

There is also the great debate between the official teaching of the church and the iconographers. In a chapter titled "On Icon Painters and the Lord of Sabaoth" from the Council of Moscow in

---

[25]Stephen Mitchell, *The Selected Poetry of Rainer Maria Rilke* (New York: Vintage, 1982), 298.

1666–1667, the patriarchy specifically orders "that from now on the image of the Lord of Sabaoth (i.e., the Father) be never painted in absurd and inappropriate ways, because nobody has ever seen the Lord of Sabaoth in the flesh." They declared it was indeed "quite absurd and inappropriate to depict . . . the Lord of Sabaoth with a gray beard and His only-begotten Son in His abdomen with a dove above them," as was a popular iconographic depiction, "because who has seen the Father as Divinity?" Despite how explicit this admonition is, according to Vladmir Andrejev, this ban was "taken by the Church as a mere formality for several centuries" and was never actually accepted by the Church; and "generation after generation of icon painters continue to use it." Part of the justification for it is that even Adam and Eve "heard the sound of the Lord God walking in the garden in the cool of the day" (Gen. 3:8), and Jacob saw and even wrestled with God. Many prophets too: Moses saw God's "afterward"; Isaiah "saw the Lord sitting upon a throne, high and lifted up; and the train of his robe filled the temple" (Is. 6:1). The argument is that none of them saw God's essence, only an image and likeness. Still, there it is: the Council of Moscow teaches that "the Father has no body and the Son was not born through the flesh from the Father before all times . . . because the birth was not corporeal, but inexpressible and incomprehensible."[26]

Even earlier in church history, in the late fourth century there had been the great controversy among the desert monks of Egypt for a similar reason. This is a time when the learned Greeks began to infiltrate the communities of simple peasant monks. In his yearly letter, Theophilus, the bishop of Alexandria, condemned what he called the heresy of anthropomorphism—that is, conceiving of God in crudely human materialistic terms. Even though Adam was made in the image and likeness of God, Theophilus insisted that doesn't mean that God has actual hands and feet and a face, nor a human

---

[26]Vladmir Andrejev, "Concerning the Single Deity in the Depiction of the Lord of Sabaoth," unpublished essay, 1–2.

form (*anthrōp morphos*) at all. This was heavily influenced by the
renowned exegete Origen who espoused a more symbolic allegorical understanding of scripture rather than a literal one, and the
influential monk and teacher Evagrius who taught that the highest
form of prayer was wordless and imageless. We hear about all this
from John Cassian, urging his monks to unceasing and imageless
prayer. There was some fear that simple folks in general, including
the monks themselves, were "baptized but not converted" from
their pagan ways; even though they were not worshipping outer
idols anymore, perhaps they were still worshipping inner ones.

We see how hard it is to resist anthropomorphizing the Divine.
I have often argued in a similar vein, that many of our notions
about God, especially God the Father, are still much more like
Zeus or one of the other Greek or Roman gods than the God to
whom Jesus introduces us. Perhaps the problem, as it occurred
again in the great iconoclastic controversy in the eighth century
when Emperor Leo III issued a similar decree to Theophilus, is in
seeing the imaging the divine in human form as a heresy rather than
seeing it merely as a stage in the evolution of consciousness and a
growth in understanding. These are images and ideas off which one
must be weaned through maturity and formation. We learn from
these events, which had both political undertows and dire social
ramifications, how strong the need is to start somewhere, with an
image or at least an idea that can be grasped, and then move from
the known to the unknown.

We see the same phenomenon among popular religiosity of the
so-called mystical traditions of Asia, Hinduism, Buddhism, and
Taoism, incidentally, where common folk are often much more
likely to practice *puja* (acts of worship) to deities than to engage in
meditation. The sad image John Cassian leaves us is of the monk
Serapion, who by all reports was a holy man in his own way, de-
livering the anguished cry, "They have taken my God from me,
and I have no one to lay hold of, nor do I know whom I should
adore or address."

APOPHATIC DEPTH IN ME

Remember the admonition of 14th century German mystic Johannes Tauler: "It is much better to have experience of the Trinity than to talk about it. We should learn to find the Trinity in ourselves, and realize how we are in a real way formed according to its image. If we want to experience this we must turn inward." And so: What is the apophatic depth of me?

There is a marvelous phrase from the twentieth-century French Orthodox theologian Paul Evdokimov. He calls Orthodox thinking an "apophatic anthropology that corresponds to apophatic theology," in which the heart/spirit is "the radiating center that suffuses all of [a human being]; at the same time it is hidden by its own depth."[27] An apophatic theology that leads to an apophatic anthropology; in other words, just as there is an apophatic depth to God, so there is an apophatic depth to me. *I too am a fathomless abyss.*

When we discover this apophatic dimension of God, we simultaneously discover the apophatic dimension of ourselves, the fine point of the soul where we are already in union with God. Sadly, this is a discovery that many of us never make.

There is a section of the Katha Upanishad that Bede Griffiths often quoted:

The self-existent one pierced the senses to look outward.
Therefore, people look toward what is without
and do not see the *antarātman—the* inner self.
Rare are those who, longing for immortality,
turn the gaze around and behold the Self.[28]

This is one of the major reasons why the anthropology of spirit, soul, and body that Bede Griffiths espoused is so important, an

---

[27] Paul Evdokimov, *Woman and the Salvation of the World: A Christian Anthropology on the Charisms of Women* (Crestwood, NY: St. Vladmir's Seminary Press, 1994), 43.
[28] See Katha Upanishad IV.1.

anthropology that is also more prominent in Eastern Christianity. The idea is that just as all created reality has a spiritual, psychological, and material dimension, so each human being is spirit, soul, and body. This is not the typical Western way to speak of Christian anthropology. We do not normally distinguish spirit from soul but speak of the human person as either body and soul or body and spirit, though we do speak of the "spiritual soul" (for example, in the Catechism of the Roman Catholic Church).

Bede claimed that this view of the human person as body, soul, and spirit was fundamental in the Bible and very clear in St. Paul.[29] As body, human nature is part of the whole physical universe. It evolves out of the physical universe, from matter and life. As soul (*psyche*), humanity is the head of the universe; it is, in a sense, matter coming into consciousness and forming an individual soul. But then, like matter itself, that soul has the potential to open to the *pneuma*, the spirit, which is the point where the human spirit opens on the Spirit of God.[30]

An apophatic theology that leads to an apophatic anthropology: just as there is an apophatic depth to God, so there is an apophatic depth to me. I too am a fathomless abyss.

When we discover this apophatic dimension of God, the next step is to discover the apophatic dimension of ourselves. Bruno says, "It is as if we had long been taught to imagine the Absolute Reality, God, outside and above us, completely separate from ourselves, and suddenly we discover this Supreme Reality within— indeed as one with our inner being, as the ultimate center of the human person."[31] This is a whole new starting point from most religious paths. The mystical, contemplative path really begins in earnest here, with this discovery—and it has been the impetus for

[29]See, for instance, 1 Thes. 5:23: *Now may the God of peace himself sanctify you completely, and may your whole spirit and soul and body be kept blameless at the coming of our Lord Jesus Christ.*

[30]Bede Griffiths, *A New Vision of Reality: Western Science, Eastern Mysticism and Christian Faith* (Springfield, IL: Templegate, 1989), 97.

[31]Bruno Barnhart, *Second Simplicity: The Inner Shape of Christianity* (New York: Paulist Press, 1999), 25.

so many who have discovered the mystical paths and contemplative practices of Asia, as well as the birth of a renewed interest in
contemplative practices among Christians. This is the pathway of
interiority and silent meditation, and the source of what is known
as the perennial philosophy.

And that leads us to this second aspect of the First Person.

3

Abyss and Ground

In the last chapter we spoke about the genuine mystery of God, the mystery that makes itself known when we swim upstream against our usual way of knowing, when our rational minds get driven to that which precedes reason and is indeed the source of reason, to the mystery that cannot be named. Now let's let the current carry us back downstream.

The apophatic aspect of the Divine is the negative side of the mystery, the fathomless abyss of the godhead. Theologian Paul Tillich calls it "the abysmal element in the ground of being." This negative side of the mystery is a very necessary part of revelation: "Without it the mystery would not be mystery," Tillich says. He recalls how the prophet Isaiah cries out in his vocational vision,

> Woe is me! I am lost,
> for I am a man of unclean lips,
> and I live among a people of unclean lips;
> yet my eyes have seen the King, the Lord of hosts! (Is. 6:5)

This is just before one of the seraphs flies to the prophet, holding a live coal with which he touches Isaiah's mouth, saying:

"Now that this has touched your lips,
your guilt has departed and your sin is blotted out."
Then [Isaiah says] I heard the voice of the Lord saying,
"Whom shall I send, and who will go for us?"
And I said, "Here am I; send me!" (Is. 6:5–8)

Tillich says that without the "I am lost" of Isaiah, God could not
have been experienced.

Notably, the commission comes *after* the theophany. Just so,
"without the 'dark night of the soul,' the mystic cannot experience
the mystery of the ground." This is the negative side of the mystery.

The *positive* side of the mystery, however, is when this abyss of
the godhead becomes manifest, when the mystery appears to be
not only an abyss but as the ground, the ground of being, and the
power of being that conquers nonbeing.[1]

You see, there is danger if we just stay in the apophatic silence
and the *via negativa*, unless and until we discover that the abyss is
also a source, a fount, a womb—the font of being.

The next step for those of us who desire to know this God of
mystery is when we discover how this fathomless abyss of the
godhead—the silence, the emptiness, the unnamable, indescribable, uncontainable—is also, as St. Bonaventure names it, a *fons
bonitatis*, a fountain of goodness, the source of all Being.

Not that Bonaventure had this in mind, but notice the similarity
in how the first chapter of *Tao te Ching* begins:

The Tao that can be named is not the eternal Tao.
The name that can be named is not the eternal name.

There's our apophatic dimension. But it doesn't stay there. It continues by saying that

---

[1] Paul Tillich, *Systematic Theology*, vol. 1 (Chicago: University of Chicago Press,
1967), 110. Tillich also makes reference to the "stigma of finitude" and the "shock
which grasps the mind when it encounters the threat of nonbeing."

The nameless is the origin of heaven and earth;
[and] named it is the mother of the ten thousand things.

So, it can be named! And when it is named, it is/becomes the Great Mother. So chapter 40 of *Tao te Ching* states:

The ten thousand things are born of being.
Being is born of emptiness.

Or perhaps in our economy we would turn it around to say: emptiness gives birth to being; and then being gives birth to the ten thousand things. Now we discover God not simply as a silent empty mystery but as Being itself.

THE METAPHYSICS OF EXODUS

Let's return to the Book of Exodus. It could be said that the Jewish scriptures and the New Testament gospels do not really have a metaphysics to them, meaning there's no philosophy in them or underlying them, strictly speaking, at least none of the more obtuse philosophical sciences as we know them. The scriptures use iconographic language, symbolic and mythical language, and so if what is contained in scripture is going to be expressed in a philosophy, in rational language, Jews and Christians will have to borrow a philosophical language.[2]

The French Thomist philosopher Etienne Gilson says something interesting in *The Spirit of Medieval Philosophy* (a book that had a huge impact on the young Thomas Merton): "We do not maintain that the text of Exodus is a revealed *definition* of God." Remember what we quoted above from Sri Aurobindo of India: the whole

---

[2]Christianity would soon borrow Greek philosophical terms, which are to some extent already embedded in the Greek language that Paul uses to draw out his anthropology in the epistles, for instance.

of scripture is an attempt, "not to define, but to characterize and present an idea, and even a detailed idea of God."[3] And so Gilson writes that even "if there is no metaphysic *in* Exodus, there is nevertheless a metaphysic *of* Exodus; and we shall see it developed in due course by the Fathers of the Church."[4] So, a philosophy—a wisdom tradition, an understanding of Absolute Reality and the created world—can be drawn and developed *from* scripture, which becomes the enterprise of the great Christian philosophers, borrowing language from the Greeks.

In order to know what God is, Moses turns to God and asks God's name, "and straightway comes the answer":

"I am who I am."
He said further,
"Thus you shall say to the Israelites,
'I am has sent me to you.' "[5]

There's no hint of metaphysics here, Gilson says. God speaks and *causa finita est*—the case is closed. "I am."

However, what the Book of Exodus has done here is "lay down the principle *from which henceforth the whole of Christian philosophy will be suspended.*" The whole of Christian philosophy is going to hang on this one phrase: "I am who am"! If this is true, then we ought to pay attention. "From this moment it is understood once and for all that *the proper name of God is Being* and that, according to the word of St. Ephrem, taken up again later by St. Bonaventure, this name denotes His very essence."[6]

This is why Thomas Aquinas, referring expressly to this text of Exodus, declares in the *Summa* that among all divine names "there

---

[3]Sri Aurobindo, *The Philosophy of the Upanishads* (Pondicherry: Sri Aurobindo Ashram Press, 1994), 18–19.
[4]Etienne Gilson, *The Spirit of Mediaeval Philosophy* (London: Sheed & Ward, 1936), 433n9. Gilson quotes it in Latin; I am quoting the NRSV. All emphases mine.
[5]*Ego sum qui sum, Ait: sic dices filiis Israel; qui est misit me ad vos;* Ex. 3:14.
[6]Gilson, *The Spirit of Mediaeval Philosophy,* 51.

is one that is eminently proper to God, namely *Qui est*—the One
Who Is because this *Qui est . . . non significat formam aliquam sed
ipsum esse.*" "The One Who Is" signifies nothing other than Being
itself.[7]

> In this principle lies an inexhaustible metaphysical fecundity.
> . . . There is but one God and this God is Being. That is the
> cornerstone of all Christian philosophy, and it was not Plato,
> it was not even Aristotle, it was Moses who put it in position.[8]

So, whereas the Asian mystical traditions and perhaps the contemplative path in general are brilliant at introducing us to the silence, the emptiness, the unnamable, indescribable, uncontainable,
the prophetic traditions' gift is in recognizing that the silence and
the emptiness is also a *fons bonitatis*, a fountain of goodness—the
Creator and the Source of all Being. This is God (or Absolute Reality) as Ground-of-Being, as the Source from which all comes forth.

"Being is born of emptiness." Again, pointing back to the practice of silent meditation, we first of all empty ourselves of all that is
"not God" and not godly with the sure hope that if we do we will
then experience God at the ground of our being, *as* the Ground
of Being. This, as we shall explore below, gives new vitality to our
spiritual lives and our lives in general. What happens *after* a period
of meditation and contemplative prayer, what flows from it, is just
as important as the prayer and meditation itself.

GOD DOES NOT EXIST

We have to make a minor but important philosophical distinction between essence and existence, in Latin *esse* versus *ens*. Simply
put, existence depends on essence, existing depends on being. An

---

[7]Thomas Aquinas, *Sum. theo.*, I, 13, II. Translation mine.
[8]Gilson, *The Spirit of Mediaeval Philosophy*, 51.

ens is an entity, a being, a thing. St. Thomas does not say that God is existence—*Deus est ens* but that God is *ipsum esse subsistens*—"the act of being itself." God is not a "thing"; God is not an entity; God is no-thing. On the other hand, every *ens*, every entity, every-one, and every "thing" that exists does so because it shares in Being—Being who is God.

We exist; God is. We are entities, we are beings; God is Being. That's why Thomas says that God is *actus purus*—the pure act of Being.

Panikkar says it this way: we tend to think of God as an *ens realissimum,* the greatest entity, the greatest being in a hierarchy of beings—like Zeus on the top of Mount Olympus! But, God is not a being at all. Instead, God is *esse ipsum*—Being itself.[9] Just drop that one little article—"a"—and everything changes. God is not a being; God is Being.

And here's how it ties in with our apophatic theology and spirituality. Nothing can be said about God that is not symbolic. There is our apophatic approach: all language about God is merely symbolic. However, the statement that God is being-itself isn't a symbolic statement: "It means what it says directly and properly."[10] Tillich had no place for any kind of metaphysics that claimed to prove the "existence" of God because, strictly speaking, God does not "exist." God *is*! God is Being-itself and Being-itself is beyond all our philosophical categories, beyond even the difference between essence and existence. Therefore, Tillich says, to argue that God exists is to deny God! "Being itself infinitely transcends every finite being. There is no proportion or gradation between the finite and the infinite. There is an absolute break, an infinite 'jump.'"[11]

On the other hand, everything finite—and this is the good news—every entity, every being, participates in Being-itself and

---

[9]Panikkar actually suggests that we shouldn't even say, "God is" but "God Am."

[10]Tillich, *Systematic Theology,* vol. 1, 238. "God is the ground of the ontological structure of being without being subject to this structure himself. God is the structure."

[11]Ibid., 205.

participates in the infinity of Being. Otherwise, it would not be. It would not have the power of being. It would be swallowed up by nonbeing, or it would never have emerged out of nonbeing in the first place.[12]

Note the word "participates." Here is a hint of our fourth element, how we join in the Dance of the Trinity from our inception. If God is Being, then we already participate in God by the very fact that we exist. Remember what Paul said in the Acts of the Apostles in his speech at the Areopagus and what this might have meant to the Greeks in Athens to whom he was speaking, and what it certainly meant to the seventh-century Syrian monk who took the name of Dionysius the Areopagite:

> Yet God is actually not far from each one of us,
> for "In him we live and move and have our being";
> as even some of your own poets have said,
> "For we are indeed his offspring."
> Being then God's offspring,
> we ought not to think that the divine being is like gold or
>   silver or stone,
> an image formed by the art and imagination. (Acts
>   17:27–28)

Bishop Robert Barron elucidates all of this clearly in one of his earliest books. God is not a competing supreme being, he writes; instead God is "the power whose very closeness to us enhances our humanity, whose proximity makes us most fully ourselves." Further, God is a "reality that can work its way into every corner of creation without ceasing to be itself," precisely because, as we have said, "God is not *a being* but the mysterious power of Being itself."[13]

Barron too mentions Tillich and how he referred to God as

---

[12]Ibid., 237.
[13]Robert Barron, *And Now I See: A Theology of Transformation* (New York: Crossroad, 1998), 203.

Grund des Seins-ground of being. *Grund* is a term also favored by the thirteenth-century Rhineland mystic Meister Eckhart and, incidentally, a notion familiar to the Hindu tradition as well, which refers to God as *brahman* or "ground of being," which we will explore shortly. And here Barron practically turns this theme into poetry, which all good theology ought to be.

> God is the underlying and sustaining source of all that is:
> God is like the rich dark earth that nurtures the foliage of
>   the garden.
> But this must mean that God is lower than all things,
> indeed, in the most dramatic way possible, at the service of
>   them all.[14]

As opposed to Zeus on a mountaintop, the *ens realissimum*, we speak instead of the humility of God. Note that the word "humility" comes from the Latin *humus*, which means "dirt or ground" and is also the root for the word "human," like Adam, whose name in Hebrew, *adamah*, also means "the creature of the earth," the one who was formed "from the dust of the ground" (Gen. 2:7). And God breathed *nephesh*—life, Being itself, into the clay—and out came a human being.

We are creatures of the *humus*: we come forth from the Ground of Being, formed from the ground of the earth. By our very existence we participate in God, like the foliage in the garden participates in the rich dark earth, "For we are indeed his offspring."

BEING, KNOWLEDGE, AND BLISS

Here the Christian tradition diverges slightly from the strictest understanding of monotheism in Judaism and Islam. What we learn

---

[14]Ibid., 143. Sense lines mine. The reader will see by my sense lines how I like to view theology as poetry.

from Jesus' relationship to God is that not only all humanity, but creation too is in relation to God because it has no existence in itself: it exists only because it is in relation to God. This is what Semitic monotheism does not recognize, and yet "the whole tradition of the universal wisdom recognizes this intimate relation between God and humanity, God and creation," as Bede Griffiths explained. In *relationship with*, mind you, not *identical with*. Just as Jesus is in relationship with the Father, so all humanity, and ultimately all creation, can be (and in some way already is): "the world is not divided; there is no separation between God and the world."[15]

Here we again have correspondence with the Hindu tradition. Bede Griffiths and his confrere and predecessor at Shantivanam, Abhishiktananda, wrestled with and meditated at great length on the Hindu concept of *advaita*-non-duality as a way to articulate the Christian experience of God. What could a Christian learn from this Indian way of understanding our relationship to Ultimate Reality? It revolves around three other Sanskrit terms, *brahman*, *atman*, and *saccidananda*.

An easy way to define *brahman* is, as we have said about God's own self, "the ground of being." Before nature takes any kind of form, there is an absolute, infinite transcendent reality that is its ground, the ground of being. This is known as *brahman*. And behind all human consciousness, before sense or any thought, there is an absolute, transcendent consciousness, which is the ground of all consciousness. This is known as *atman*. And the intuition of the Indian seers of the sacred scriptures known as the Upanishads is that the ground of being and the ground of consciousness are one and the same—*brahman ayam atman, brahman* is *atman*, the source of my consciousness is one with the ground of being; the ground of being and the ground of consciousness are the same. And so the Upanishads say, "Thou art That" (in Sanskrit, *tat tvam*

---

[15]Bede Griffiths, *Universal Wisdom: A Journey through the Sacred Wisdom of the World* (New York: HarperCollins, 1994), 430.

asi) meaning, "Thou," my consciousness, my deepest Self in its transcendent ground, is one with "That," the transcendent ground of all that exists.

Another single but compound word, which we already saw in the introduction as a possible appellative for the Trinity, is *saccidananda*,[16] which is made up of three root words: *sat* meaning "being," *cit* meaning "knowledge or consciousness," and *ananda* meaning "bliss." Johannes Tauler tells us it is better to have an experience of the Trinity than to talk about it. Well, *saccidananda* is such an experience: to have the experience of real awareness (*cit*) of Being itself (*sat*) produces bliss (*ananda*).

If and when I would come to realize that my own self comes forth from the great Self of God who is Being itself, like foliage from the loamy earth, I would experience great beatitude. I see this as part of the *scopos*-goal of our sinking into our own bodilyness in spiritual practices such as meditation, yoga, purification ("sweat") lodges, even in exerting ourselves in physical activities such as dance and exercise: to have an ecstatic experience that is also *en*static, both out of the ordinary while deep within our own being.

THE JEWISH MYSTICAL TRADITION

This way of thinking, being, and practicing is not without its resonance among our Jewish brothers and sisters, particularly in the more mystical side of Jewish spirituality. There is, for instance, this from a Polish Jewish teacher named Kalynomous Kalmish Shapira, which goes beautifully with Bishop Barron's notion of how God is "a reality that can work its way into every corner of creation." Rabbi Shapira was called "the Rebbe of the Warsaw Ghetto" during World War II and was himself killed in the Shoah. He wrote several works that wrestle with the difficulty of having

---

[16]There are various spellings of this word in transliteration, but I shall use this one regularly.

faith in God's justice under such circumstances, drawing answers from the Kabbalah tradition. He said:

> I may not be able to see it right now, but the Holy One fills all creation; being, itself, is made of God; you and I—everything is made of God. Even the grains of sand beneath my feet, the whole world is included and, therefore, utterly dissolved within God—while I, in my stubborn insistence on my own autonomy and independence, only succeed in banishing myself from any possibility of meaning whatsoever.[17]

Our move from autonomous individuality to full personhood involves us being in relationship, with God as well as with others and with creation itself. If we stubbornly insist on autonomy and independence, from God, from others, from creation itself—all that exists—we banish ourselves from any possibility of meaning. I find great similarity between this teaching and that of Teilhard: "To be fully ourselves it is in the direction of convergence with all the rest, that we must advance—toward the 'other.' The goal of ourselves, the acme of our originality, is not our individuality but our *person*: and according to the evolutionary structure of the world, we can only find our person by uniting together."[18]

Arthur Green, a contemporary rabbi and writer on Jewish mysticism, states it plainly: "God *is* Being," and then goes on to explain how the Kabbalah tradition loves to meditate on the hidden messages in letters and numbers. For example, if one were to take the four letters of the great tetragrammaton, God's revealed name in the Book of Exodus, Y-H-W-H, in reverse order, it spells the H-W-Y-H, pronounced *hawayah*, a Hebrew word which means "existence." Rabbi Green writes that the meaning of this is that "all that is, exists within God." Plain and simple.

---

[17] *B'nei Makhsahva Tova*, p. 33, #14 (Hebrew) Jerusalem, 1989; trans. Lawrence Kushner. Used with permission.

[18] Pierre Teilhard de Chardin, *Phenomenon of Man* (New York: Harper Colophon, 1975), 263.

And when we turn those letters around again and make them into the Divine Name, something of mystery gets added: "The infinitely varied cosmos gives way to a single Being, One in whose presence we feel ourselves standing."[19] *In whom we live and move and have our being.*

Being is born of emptiness. And now let's explore how the ten thousand things are born of Being.

[19]Arthur Green, *Ehyeh: A Kabbalah for Tomorrow* (Woodstock, VT: Jewish Lights, 2003), 2.

4

Great Mother

At the end of the Book of Deuteronomy there is an enigmatic line in a canticle that in the Camaldolese tradition we sing every Saturday morning. One day I finally paid attention to it. It sings, "You were unmindful of the Rock that bore you; you forgot the God who gave you birth" (Dt. 32:18).[1] The rock that bore you; the God who gave you birth. Add those lines to the scene in the Gospel of John when Nicodemus comes to Jesus at night and asks him: "How can anyone be born after having grown old? Can one enter a second time into the mother's womb and be born?" (Jn. 3:4). We'll return to that story shortly.

First, recall and retain what we said in the first chapter, that the word "person" does not necessarily mean a human, nor is it the same as an individual. "Person" means a knot in a rope of relationships. "An 'I' implies a 'thou'—and a he and a she and an it and a we and an us and all together; otherwise it's not a person." It goes without saying that the name, the inspired metaphor, "Father" holds a privileged place in our tradition. It was how Jesus described his relationship with his God. Remember that even after the resur-

---

[1] See Cyprian Consiglio, *The God Who Gave You Birth: A Spirituality of Kenosis* (Collegeville, MN: Liturgical Press, 2021), where I touch on this theme, which will be explored in more depth in the present work.

rection Jesus tells Mary Magdalene, "I am ascending to my Father and your Father, to my God and your God" (Jn. 20:16). So when we are speaking about the First Person of the Trinity, we don't want to dismiss the masculine images for God out of hand.

However, it's important to bring out the feminine aspects of this Person, as uncomfortable as it may be for those of us who are used to the masculine language (and perhaps others who even carry a certain suspicion about a "feminist agenda"). My own problem with female images of God has been that it has often felt as if we were trying to set up another idol next to the one we already have, an old woman, perhaps a venerable crone, next to the old man on the throne. And that winds up being yet another image that I need to dismantle, another form I have to get beyond.

MATERNAL IMAGES IN SCRIPTURE

Our rare biblical images of God as mother, like "Father in heaven," tend still to carry a sense of God outside of us, as "Father in heaven" does. For example, the canticle in Deuteronomy 32:

As an eagle stirs up its nest,
and hovers over its young;
as it spreads its wings, takes them up,
and bears them aloft on its pinions,
the Lord alone guided him;
no foreign god was with him.
He set him atop the heights of the land,
and fed him with produce of the field;
he nursed him with honey from the crags,
with oil from flinty rock;
curds from the herd, and milk from the flock,
with fat of lambs and rams. (32:11–14)

Even though it is full of the pronoun "he," this is a very maternal nurturing image. There is an echo of this in Psalm 36: "How pre-

cious is your steadfast love, O God! All people may take refuge
in the shadow of your wings" (36:7). This is similar to the image
in Isaiah 31:5:

> Like birds hovering overhead,
> so the Lord of hosts will protect Jerusalem;
> he will protect and deliver it,
> he will spare and rescue it.

Jesus himself seems to allude to this passage in Matthew 23 and
Luke 13 when he laments over Jerusalem crying out, "How often
would I have gathered your children together as a hen gathers her
brood under her wings" (Mt. 23:37, Lk. 13:34).

    Then there is this beautiful tender maternal image in the Book
of the prophet Hosea:

> Yet it was I who taught Ephraim to walk,
> I took them up in my arms;
> but they did not know that I healed them.
> I led them with cords of human kindness,
> with bands of love.
> I was to them like those
> who lift infants to their cheeks.
> I bent down to them and fed them. (Hos. 11:3–4)

And then there are the particularly visceral images in this canticle
from the prophet Isaiah:

> Rejoice with Jerusalem, and be glad for her,
> all you who love her;
> rejoice with her in joy,
> all you who mourn over her—
> that you may nurse and be satisfied
> from her consoling breast;
> that you may drink deeply with delight
> from her glorious bosom.

For thus says the Lord:
I will extend prosperity to her like a river,
and the wealth of the nations like an overflowing stream;
and you shall nurse and be carried on her arm,
and dandled on her knees.
As a mother comforts her child,
so I will comfort you. (Is. 66:10–14)

That canticle is actually mentioned in the Catechism of the Catholic Church when affirming the use of maternal images for God, along with the verse from Psalm 131: "But I have calmed and quieted my soul, like a weaned child with its mother; my soul is like the weaned child that is with me" (v. 2).

Here's what the Catechism says about God as mother: "God's parental tenderness can also be expressed by the image of motherhood, which emphasizes God's immanence, the intimacy between Creator and creature."[2] Again, this is not something I was ever taught in all my years of Catholic education growing up. That ought to be no surprise since it only gets one line in the entire Catechism with no further expansion. God as maternal doesn't just mean nurturing, from outside, but also an active presence within us, immanent and intimate. How might this change our understanding of the Divine, if we were to think of God as immanent and intimate?

THE OUROBORIC

This quote from the late Trappist monk and spiritual teacher Thomas Keating points us to where we are going with all this: "The primary issue for the human family at its present level of evolutionary development is to become fully human. But that means discovering our connectedness to God, which was repressed

---

[2] *Catechism*, #239.

somewhere in early childhood."[3] This is the core of my argument: we need to evolve!

But in order to evolve, we need to recover something that we left behind, an energy, a dynamism. It is vitally important for us to do this at both a micro and a macro level, a kind of *ressourcement*, back to the source, *ad fontes*, individually and as a human race. We need to take a step back in order to move forward, to recover what we left behind so that we have the energy to face the future.

And what we have left behind is the immanence of God; what we've left behind is the Mother.

Transpersonal psychologist Michael Washburn's best-known book is called *The Ego and the Dynamic Ground*, and let's also keep those words in our mind as we go forward.[4] The "ego" of course refers to us, with no negative meaning attached. It is simply our "I" sense, without which we would not be able to be in relationship at all. The "dynamic ground" in the title, on the other hand, refers to God. Not only is God the Ground of Being, but that ground is dynamic, that is, God is dynamic.

The ouroboros (or uroborus) is an ancient circular symbol that depicts a snake or a dragon eating its own tail. It's a symbol found in ancient Egyptian iconography and in the Greek magical tradition, as well as in alchemy. It is often interpreted as a symbol for the eternal cyclic renewal of life, death, and rebirth. Jungians see it as representing the pre-egoic "dawn state," the undifferentiated infancy experience of humankind in general as well as the individual child, because our first experience of being and life in the womb is ouroboric, all-inclusive, with no distinct sense of a difference between me and everything else, the mother's body or Absolute Reality itself.

So our mother's womb is actually our first experience of Absolute Reality, of God, since there is no clear sense of a difference between

---

[3]Thomas Keating, *Invitation to Love*, in *Foundations for Centering Prayer and the Christian Contemplative Life* (New York: Continuum, 2006), 164.

[4]Michael Washburn, *The Ego and the Dynamic Ground: A Transpersonal Theory of Human Development* (Albany: State University of New York Press, 1995).

my mother's womb and the Ground of Being either, the *dynamic* ground. This gives us a sense of physical and spiritual dynamism, because there is no clear sense of a difference between the spiritual and psychic, and no sense of a difference between what is sacred and what is not. This is the ouroboric experience. Therefore, if this is true, our first experience of the Divine is actually archetypally feminine, more maternal than paternal, since our birth mother is our first icon of Absolute Reality and the Divine. Like the *Tao te Ching* and Carl Jung before him, Michael Washburn refers to this experience as "the Great Mother." And Panikkar suggests that "we might ask ourselves if calling God Father and Mother constitutes an anthropomorphism," imaging God in human form, or if, on the contrary, calling our parents "father" and "mother" might not actually be a *theo*morphism—projecting onto our parents our experience of God![5]

As opposed to others in his field, Washburn assumes at least the seed of an ego, a sense of an "I" in the womb, and our trajectory from birth on is toward becoming and fully realizing that "I," that person. (Keep in mind here, again, the important difference between individual and person.) My confrere Bruno suggested that this was the foundational gift of Western Christian thought as compared with Asian thought, because it is Western Christianity that gave birth to the idea of the autonomous person, a separate self with individual rights. It is from this that any form of human rights and social justice that the world knows is conceived, and so we should rejoice in it. But the movement toward autonomy also weans us from the warm embrace of mother, in many ways, and separates us from the dynamism of the Ground.

Washburn reinterprets what Freud called the Oedipal Complex by suggesting that at a certain stage of development the child discovers the "other," who is usually symbolized by the father. In what since ancient times was the normative family unit, whereas

---

[5]Raimon Panikkar, *Christophany: The Fullness of Man,* trans. Alfred DiLascia (Maryknoll, NY: Orbis Books, 2004), 91.

even after weaning from the breast the infant still has an emotional if not physical enmeshment in the mother, the "father" is the first someone who is experienced as "not me." Not only that, but the "father" can both be intimate (with the mother) and yet be independent. The father can leave the home all day and still come home to enjoy mother's affection. So the child starts to imitate the father, weaning itself away from the enmeshment in mother's body and affection, attempting to find the right balance between intimacy and independence. This is simply the natural trajectory of growth toward the establishment of an autonomous, generative self, becoming an other.

This could also serve as a metaphor for human consciousness in general from an evolutionary standpoint, because we could also see this as what humanity has gone through in its own evolution of consciousness. Perhaps at some point in our evolution human beings started to image and relate to God as wholly Other, wholly outside (and wholly masculine), as we as a race moved toward ever greater autonomy and independence, meanwhile forgetting the Ground from which we came, "the God who gave us birth."

The problem, at a micro level, is that as we break away from our birth mother in our striving toward independence and autonomy, we also break away from the Dynamic Ground, mainly psychologically, but that psycho-emotional move has physical as well as spiritual ramifications. Whereas the early ouroboric experience knew no differentiation between body, soul, and spirit, as the traces of that all-inclusive unitive experience slowly start to diminish, we slowly lose the sense of unity with the natural world around us. (This is worse in some than in others. Some children are lucky enough to grow up immersed in nature and the natural world. Others are preternaturally inclined that way.) And since the dynamic ground has also been a spiritual experience—the Dynamic Ground as our own power, at least power we share in—Washburn suggests that we also lose the dynamism of the spiritual (and the Spirit). We leave behind both our body and our spirit, and we become solely a "mental ego" instead. At a physical level (how many times have I heard this in contemporary spiritual circles!) people will talk about *having* a body instead of *being* one. At a spiritual level, on the other hand, when we are cut off from the Ground, the dynamism of the spiritual dimension gets lost almost completely. We end up with René Descartes's *Cogito ergo sum*–"I think therefore I am," the definitive description of the self in modern Western culture, even of modern world culture.[6]

Now the thinking, rational self is seen as being separate from the rest of the universe, individuals, not persons-in-relationship, cut off not only from our embedded-ness in the natural world and relationship with our own bodies, cut off not only from an authentic immersion in social life and a sense of real belonging to the collective, but also cut off from the Dynamic Ground of the spiritual realm. We experience ourselves as self-contained imper-meable units without a real sense of relation to—let alone unity with—other independent units, other people and the natural world, or the Divine.

Not only is this not so, unreal, it is unhealthy for us and those around us to proceed as if this is true, or real. And, as we shall see, there is an evolution, a growth particularly in our spiritual develop-ment that we cannot make unless we overcome this independence.

WOMB OF BEING, WOMB OF MERCY

Our prenatal experience is an icon, even more, a physical em-bodiment of the relationship that we had with God and the entire universe at our inception, a relationship we can and are meant to regain, with God and the entire universe. To become fully human we need to rediscover this connectedness which, as Thomas Keat-

---

[6]Richard Tarnas, *Passion of the Western Mind: Understanding the Ideas That Have Shaped Our World View* (New York: Ballantine Books, 1991), 275. See also Carter Phipps, *Evolutionaries: Unlocking the Spiritual and Cultural Potential of Science's Greatest Idea* (New York: HarperCollins, 2012), 158.

ing said, was repressed somewhere in early childhood. We need to regain that if we are to evolve as individuals—and as a people. What I am positing is that the next phase in our evolution needs to be a kind of regression before we can transcend—or an "inscendence," to use the word coined by Thomas Berry, that is needed before we can evolve, and we will see more on that later. Here we are at the first moment, and if this holds true, then Absolute Reality (God) is experienced more as maternal than paternal, the womb of Being, the Great Mother. Our first real experience of Absolute Reality is the Ground from which we come forth, hence why we need to recover God-as-Mother, a *unitive* experience of God, a oneness with God, in God's womb, which is also an experience of oneness with creation itself.

Recall once again the scene in the Gospel of John when Jesus told Nicodemus that "no one can see the kingdom of God without being born from above." When Nicodemus asked him how anyone could "be born after having grown old? Can one enter a second time into the mother's womb and be born?" Jesus answered, yes and no: born of the flesh, no; but "what is born of the Spirit is spirit" (Jn. 3:1–6). So there is a second birth, a *spiritual* birth that needs to happen in us.

Remember too that the Aramaic word for "mercy" Jesus would have used throughout the gospels is *rahamim*, which is related to the Hebrew word *rachum*, a word that describes what a woman feels toward the child she carries in her womb. It's the word used in the Book of Exodus when "the Lord passed in front of Moses and proclaimed, 'The Lord, the Lord God, compassionate [*rachum*] and gracious, slow to anger, and abounding in lovingkindness and truth'" (Ex. 34:6). It comes from the same Semitic root as the Arabic words that begin every *surah* of the Qur'an: *Bismillah ir-rahman ir-rahim*: "In praise of Allah all merciful and compassionate," from the Arabic word *rachma*—mercy.

The womb of Being is also the womb of compassion, the womb of mercy, as Thomas Merton wrote, "mercy within mercy within mercy."[7] The merciful God who is both immanent and intimate.

My own connection with the image of God as Mother is through the Brief Rule of Saint Romuald of Ravenna, the father of my own monastic congregation. He ends his advice for hermits by saying that we should first of all "stand before God with the attitude of one who stands before the emperor," a very masculine image from one who actually knew the emperor pretty well. But then he adds a feminine image, that we should also "sit waiting like a chick who tastes nothing and eats nothing but what his mother gives him."

There is a marvelous passage from Clement of Alexandria, in which he mixes the metaphors: "In his ineffable majesty God is our Father, but in the comfort he extends to us he has become our mother. Yes, the Father in his love became a woman, and the son whom he brought forth from himself is strong proof of this."[8]

Even more I love how the Irish theologian Diarmuid O'Murchu expressed it: birthing is actually God's primary activity, "radiant in every aspect of creation, including its paradoxical features of birth–death–rebirth."[9] Again, with all due respect for the inspired metaphor that is "Father," like O'Murchu I am suggesting that the idea of a prodigiously creative mother figure may be an even better image of the primordial creative source for our times than an outstanding patriarchal male, or at least a "Father who becomes a woman."

In some way Mary the mother of Jesus represents this. Like the birthing experience of every mother and child, so in and through Mary, "the womb of God and the womb of the universe are one." So each year the seasons of Advent and Christmas become "perpetual reminders to us that we have been birthed from the womb of a birthing universe."[10] An ultimate step, which we will meet again with Mary in the last chapter, is to realize that our task is to

---

[7]Thomas Merton, *The Sign of Jonas* (New York: Harcourt Brace, 1953), 362.

[8]*Quis dives alvetur?* 38–39: PG 9, 641–644, in *The Word in Season*, vol. 1, Thursday after Epiphany to the Baptism of the Lord (Villanova, PA: Augustinian Press, 2001), 124.

[9]Diarmuid O'Murchu, *Incarnation: A New Evolutionary Threshold* (Maryknoll, NY: Orbis Books, 2007), 199.

[10]Ibid.

continue this creative process of birthing.[11] The unitive experience becomes the unitive way of life.

THE SACRIFICE
OF OUR AUTONOMY

Recall again that beautiful passage from Rebbe Kalynomous that ends with the words "while I, in my stubborn insistence on my own autonomy and independence, only succeed in banishing myself from any possibility of meaning whatsoever." The next step is a kind of regression. In order to fulfill our humanness to the highest degree at some point we must recover the dynamic power of the Ground. We have to sacrifice our autonomy and go back to the Great Mother, reestablish our link with the dynamic ground of being and consciousness that we at one time, though unconsciously, experienced as our *own* dynamic ground, in order to move now from individuality to full personhood, from "I" to "we" in order to be fully human and grow into the likeness of God—both as individual human beings and as a race. This will demand a kind of death for us, a *kenosis*, a sacrifice of the ways of thinking and living to which we have grown accustomed. As the Jungian psychoanalyst James Hillman wrote, "At this moment of transition we cannot advance until we have first retreated enough inward and backward so that the unconscious . . . within us can catch up with us."[12] This too is our kenosis, the movement inward and backward. We shall explore this more in depth below.

So, how do we do what Johannes Tauler reminds us to do and have an experience of the Trinity rather than just talk about it? We should learn to find the Trinity in ourselves and realize how we are in a real way formed according to its image. If we want to

---

[11]Ibid., 202.
[12]James Hillman, "Senex and Puer," in *Puer Papers*, ed. James Hillman (Dallas: Spring Publications, 1989), 38.

experience this, we must turn inward and backward, away from the activities of both our exterior and interior faculties, away from all imaginations and all the notions we have acquired from outside ourselves, and sink and lose ourselves in the depths.

Perhaps in this experience of turning inward, we won't get lost in our inwardness but instead once again meet the Great Mother in the dynamic power of the *Grund des Seins*—sacrifice our autonomy and be born again with revitalized spiritual energy and knowledge of our unity with God and all creation that is groaning and in agony while we work this out. This will be part of our exploration of the remaining three dimensions, all of which are manifestations of that Ground in us and in creation.

Before we move into the Second Person let's meditate on how we have articulated our rediscovery of God so far, and of how we are in a real way formed according to God's image. God is a fathomless abyss from which issues forth Being itself as if from the womb of a mother. Just so, there is a fathomless abyss to me, the ultimate point of my being where my existence is continuously pouring forth from the womb of Being. This is why we make the inward journey of contemplative prayer and meditation, not only to rest in that immanent presence, but to be born again, energized, and regenerated.

5

Word (and Wisdom)
Out of Silence

The genuine mystery appears when reason gets driven beyond itself, back to its ground, back to the abyss, when reason is driven back to that which precedes it. This is the negative side of the mystery, the abyss of the ground of Being that Tillich says is necessary in revelation because without this negative side, "the mystery would not be mystery. . . . Without the 'dark night of the soul,' the mystic cannot experience the mystery of the ground."

The positive side of the mystery is when this abyss becomes manifest in actual revelation. This is when the mystery appears not only as an abyss but as the ground, the ground of consciousness, but even more, in Tillich's thought, the ground of being, the power of being that conquers nonbeing. This is when the mystery gets expressed "in symbols and myths which point to the depth of reason and its mystery."[1]

Ignatius of Antioch said, "There is only one God, revealed by Jesus Christ his Son who is his Word sprung from the silence."[2]

---

[1] Paul Tillich, *Systematic Theology,* vol. 1 (Chicago: University of Chicago Press, 1967), 111–112.

[2] Ignatius of Antioch, *Letter to the Magnesians,* 8, 2 (SC 10, 102), quoted in Olivier

This too is the genius of the West, or of the prophetic traditions in general—to recognize that the Silence speaks. The so-called "East," and the contemplative path in general, tends to go to the One, to the Silence, and stay there as if re-entering the warm womb of the Mother, rather than engaging the dynamic feminine spirit who we already saw hints of in the Great Mother. The Silence speaks one Word and many words—music, science, civilization, creation, evolution, beauty, service. And this is the Second Movement—from the Silence to the Word.

The first chapter of *Tao te Ching* starts by telling us that "The Tao that can be named is not the eternal Tao. / The name that can be named is not the eternal name." But then it continues by saying that "the nameless is the origin of heaven and earth; and when it is named it is the mother of the ten thousand things." So it can be named, and when it is named it is/becomes the Great Mother. We could also say, from our tradition, that when it is named it is/becomes the Word, and/or maybe even better, Wisdom.

However, there is a mystical realm of this Word and Wisdom that is still silent, and this is our bridge from the Silence to what lies next. Panikkar says that perhaps this realm is poetical and metaphysical:

> . . . a word uttered by Being, which is the mediator to think-ing but is not (yet?) thinking. An entire human tradition East and West speaks of silence, emptiness, nothingness, the third eye, ignorance, unknowing. . . . This speaking, this *logos*, is the mediator between Being and Thinking, and we are aware of it with an awareness that is not (yet?) understanding.[3]

Here is a hint, by the way, of why I am so fond of the *Tao te Ching* as an alternative way of expressing our understanding of the Sec-

---

Clement, *The Roots of Christian Mysticism: Texts from the Patristic Era with Commentary*, 2nd ed. (Hyde Park, NY: New City Press, 1993), 36.

[3]Raimon Panikkar, *Rhythm of Being: The Unbroken Trinity* (Maryknoll, NY: Orbis Books, 2010), 149.

ond Person of the Trinity, Word and Wisdom: because Taoism reverences and expresses this realm better than anything I have encountered, the mystical realm of the Word before it gets limited and concretized by our concepts, our "imaginations and all the notions we have acquired from outside ourselves."

LECTIO DIVINA

From the Christian monastic tradition comes the practice of *lectio divina,* which is very dear to monks. Here, Word and Wisdom come together in silence.

In one version of the practice the chosen scripture passage is read four different times. Each reading corresponds to one of four levels of meaning. The tradition of differing layers of meaning in scripture seems to have started with the great third-century exegete Origen, who taught that just as the human person is body, soul, and spirit, so there is a somatic, psychic, and spiritual meaning to scripture, a literal, a moral and a spiritual meaning. From Gregory the Great on, the literal and moral meanings were retained, but the spiritual sense gets divided into the allegorical and anagogical senses. There is a further application of this practice suggested by the late theologian Ewert Cousins that the four readings and meanings also correspond to four ever-deeper levels of consciousness in the psyche.[4]

The first reading is *lectio* itself, and it corresponds to the literal meaning of the text, the time and place, the actual event. This corresponds to our ordinary consciousness and the senses. Origen compares scripture to an almond, and for him the literal meaning, like the letter of the Law, is the bitter rind that kills and must be rejected. This teaching, perhaps overstated and pursued exclusively,

---

[4]Ewert Cousins, *Christ of the Twenty-first Century* (New York: Continuum, 1998). Note that instead of the normal order of the meanings—literal, allegorical, moral, anagogical—he puts moral before symbolic, an arrangement I find very satisfying.

got Origen into trouble with the hierarchy of the Church. But Origen's intuition holds true: if we try to reduce the divine meaning to the external significance of the words only—likewise if we take every narrative literally as if we were reading a history or science book—the Word will return to its secret dwelling.

The second reading is called *meditatio.* "Meditation" here is used more in a Western sense than in an Asian way, meaning ruminating on a text, thinking about it, and expanding on it through the imagination. Maybe even quietly reading and repeating the words, mumbling them to oneself, as in Psalm 1:2, which shouldn't be translated "meditating" on the Lord's teaching day and night, as we've come to know meditation, but "murmuring" it. Think of Ignatian mental prayer in this way. This corresponds to the moral (sometimes called the tropological) meaning. Origen taught that this ethical teaching is like the protective shell of the almond, and before we can break through to the deeper layers of meaning, an outer purification is required. Every scripture passage makes a demand on us; there is something for us to do, a conversion and an action.

Then comes *oratio,* prayer. Especially salient for the preacher, this level corresponds to the symbolic, allegorical mind, the realm of archetypes, reliving the great myths and rituals of humankind. This is also the realm of ritual and mythical language. Cousins thought that it was very important for us to rediscover this rich realm of symbols as part of our spiritual heritage, re-appropriate our symbolic imagination, and rediscover the realm of religious symbols, both in literature, sacred or otherwise, and in ritual.[5]

In the liturgical tradition of the Roman church there is a subtle choreography to the ritual that speaks to this level of meaning. Immediately after the readings from scripture there comes the Universal Prayer or Prayer of the Faithful, prayers of intercession.

---

[5]According to Cousins, the moral meaning corresponds to the Freudian superego, the self-critical conscience that reflects standards set from outside of us; and the allegorical level is the realm of Jungian psychoanalysis and the collective unconscious.

As the General Instruction on the Roman Missal describes this moment, this is when "the people *respond* . . . to the Word of God."[6]
There are certainly generic versions of the intercessory prayers that
can be used at any time, but attentive liturgists often create specific
bidding prayers that flow right from the scriptures we have just
heard. In other words, the Word of God teaches us how to pray,
what to pray for, how to focus our prayer.

This is also how *oratio* works in private prayer; the scripture
reading, the Word of God, teaches us how to pray, what to pray
for, how to focus our prayer. Since the next reading will lead us
to *contemplatio,* what we might think of as meditation more in
the Asian sense—going from expanded thought to a one-pointed
consciousness—I often recommend that folks end this *oratio* stage
by coming up with a kernel of a phrase drawn from the scripture
reading, the shortest prayer possible to use as a prayer word, a kind
of mantra, to lead into meditation proper. So here we are now
moving in the other direction, to the one-pointed consciousness
of contemplative prayer rather than expanding on our thoughts
through our imagination.

Finally comes *contemplatio,* which corresponds to the mystical (or anagogical) meaning. In modern parlance this would be
called integral or mystical consciousness, what Hinduism calls
turiya—pure unitary consciousness beyond words and images.
This corresponds also to what the ancients called pure prayer, the
prayer of silence, the prayer of the heart. For Origen this is when
the spiritual kernel is reached, and for him this is all that matters,
when the soul feeds on the mysteries of divine wisdom. This again
is what raised suspicion of Origen's teaching, that he dismissed the
other meanings out of hand. Without disregarding the other levels
of meaning, it is this level that returns us to the beginning, to the
Silence from which the Word comes forth.

If our friend Rabbi Kushner, along with Gershom Scholem and

---

[6] *General Instruction of the Roman Missal,* from *The Roman Missal,* English Translation According to the Third Typical Edition (Collegeville: Liturgical Press, 2001), 69.

Mendel Torum of Rhymenov, is correct, this last may actually be the first—the seed that we unpack, and all the other levels of meaning are interpretations of that mystical silence. And in the practice of *lectio divina*, we are swimming upstream against logic back to the source, back to the seed, back to the sound of sheer silence.

There is a similar teaching in the Sufi tradition of Islam, though probably held in suspect by regular observance Muslims. It was described in a poetic way in the novel *The Forty Rules of Love* by Elik Shafak. He says that there are four levels of insight to the Holy Qur'an, and each reader comprehends it on a different level in tandem with the depth of their understanding. "The first level is the outer meaning and it is the one that the majority of the people are content with. Those who swim close to the surface are content with the outer meaning of the Qur'an. Many people are like that," Shafak says. "The second one is deeper than the first," an inner level but still close to the surface. The next level, in Arabic *batīn*, is the inner of the inner. "As your awareness expands, so does your grasp of the Qur'an. But for that to happen you need to take the plunge." And then comes a fourth level which "is so deep it cannot be put into words and is therefore bound to remain indescribable. The fourth level is unspeakable. . . . There is a stage after which language fails us. When you step into the zone of love, you won't need language."[7]

Just as we might say that time flows out of eternity—and we want to stay at the place where this is happening, like meditating at the source of the Ganges—so something flows out of the Silence. And perhaps we might say that the contemplative life and contemplative practice ask us to spend as much time as possible there at the source, in the brackish water where time flows out of eternity (Panikkar coins the word *tempiternity*), in that realm of the word that is not (yet?) thinking and the awareness that is not (yet?) understanding. Again, though, this may be a danger in contemplative life and practice—that we return to the warm silence of the

---

[7]Elif Shafak, *The Forty Rules of Love* (New York: Penguin, 2011), 50, 197–198, 220.

Great Mother and stay there, inert, basking in our re-absorption.

I am suggesting that both are true: we need to return to the Silence first before we move forward. Then, however, move on we must, from the Silence, because there is something that flows from the Silence.

GOD SPEAKS TO HUMANITY

Bede Griffiths wrote that from the beginning of the world "we human beings have known ourselves to be in the presence of mystery." And humanity has expressed this sense of mystery in myths and in legends; we have approached this mystery by prayer and sacrifice; and we have tried to apprehend this mystery by thought. However, "at a certain point in history the Mystery *chose to reveal itself.* It manifested itself by signs and wonders to a particular people." This is what we call the scandal of particularity, the revelation to Abraham and his seed. The Mystery "declared its will through the voice of the Prophets. It was revealed as a Person whose will is justice and whose nature is love." Then finally—and here Bede is obviously speaking as a Christian—"It appeared on earth in human nature and revealed in that human nature the destiny to which [all people] had through all the centuries aspired."[8]

From the perspective of the prophetic traditions and Christianity specifically, it is necessary to understand how important our belief is that God speaks to humanity. This is the salient characteristic element of revealed religion. God is not content to be searched for by humanity. The whole of the Bible shows us the divine initiative. It was not Israel that chose God, but God who chose Israel. John the Beloved Disciple notes it through love: "We love because he first loved us" (1 Jn. 4:19). Augustine says, or says that God says,

---

[8]Bede Griffiths, *The Golden String: An Autobiography* (Springfield, IL: Templegate, 1980), 183.

"You would not search if I had not already searched for you first."

The same can be said about the primordial reality of the Second Person of the Trinity. God is not only Someone who *listens* to me: God is first of all Someone who *speaks* to me.[9] This is the hallmark of the prophetic traditions or revealed religion.

When I refer to the "prophetic traditions" I principally mean Judaism, Christianity, and Islam. In this day and age I find this to be a more inclusive and much needed replacement for the phrase "Judeo-Christian." Our three traditions have much in common, a commonality that needs to be exploited rather than constantly falling back on what a Muslim colleague of mine who works intensely in the field of interreligious dialogue refers to as the "narcissism of minor differences." What the prophetic traditions have in common is that they are, first of all, marked by a revealed word, a revelation. Further, and flowing from that, we share a conviction that God uses history, and even intervenes in it, and so time is not an accident but a sacrament, which we will deal with later.

This notion of God's self-revealing through revelation is even more emphatic and literal in Islam. For instance, the Arabic word *qur'an* simply means "reading" or "recitation." The Arabic copy that a Muslim uses today is thought to be an exact replica of a heavenly prototype, dictated word by word to the Prophet Muhammad; it is seen as the eternal and uncreated word of God incarnate. Whereas Christians say the Word was made flesh in Jesus, in Islam the Word becomes the Qur'an, so the book itself is more like a consecrated host than like our Bible. One goes through an ablution before opening the book; you never put anything on top of it; you technically never sell it. (You can imagine what a heinous scandal it was for the American soldiers to desecrate a Qur'an at Abu Ghraib prison.) The Qur'an is not only the basis of religion, ethics, and morals; it is the textbook that a Muslim uses, or could use, to study language, science, theology, and law.

---

[9]Mariano Magrassi, *Bibbia e preghiera*, my translation, in Bose, *Letture dei giorni* (Casale Monferrato: Edizioni Piemme, 2000), 125–126.

Christians understand revelation as inspiration, the divine mind working through human consciousness; the Muslim understanding of revelation (*wahy*) is much more like dictation. The contents and even the word forms are divine; hence the importance of Arabic. The process is described as being sent down from heaven as an archetype to a passive recipient to whom God communicates his thought and will. And then the recipient is sent forth to announce the message—hence "prophet."

So, Muhammad on Mount Hira receives the word directly. Many Muslims will not abide with any suggestion of there being strata of different chronology or levels of interpretation as we suggested above in the Sufi version of *lectio*, just as there are some Christians who will not abide with anything but a strict fundamentalist historical interpretation of the Bible.

But how does God "speak" to us? Is it always in words that can be written down or recorded?

THE DIVINE ABYSS MANIFESTING

I must tell a story that happened in Christology class in my first year of seminary. The professor was a stately Irish monsignor, and I confess at this particular moment I was barely paying attention. But something he said suddenly caught my ear—I don't remember what—and I shot my hand up in class. If I had thought twice, I might not have asked the question, but I am very glad I did. It may seem like a basic theological question, but I have consequently asked this of crowds all over the world and have found that most people cannot answer it, perhaps because they have never thought of it. I asked, "But, Monsignor, who was the Second Person of the Trinity before Jesus was born?" And the good monsignor turned to me and said, rather fiercely, words that I will never forget: "The Word, man! The Word!"

This is who we are in search of here, now: the Second Person of the Trinity before Jesus was born. We easily think of Jesus as a person since he was a human being. But the Palestinian Jewish man Jesus did not exist eternally. Jesus was and is the Second Person of the Trinity incarnate, made flesh. But who is the Person behind that person? The Word. And soon we will stretch that to include Wisdom: the Word and Wisdom of God is the Second Person of the Trinity.

Paul Tillich distinguished six different meanings of the phrase "Word of God." The last three are the ones we recognize: the Word as a name for Jesus as the Christ, Logos or Word who becomes a being in history; the document, namely, the Bible; and the message of the church, the proclamation, its preaching and teaching. Those are the meanings of "Word" to which we are accustomed.

First and foremost, however, put simply, the Second Person of the Trinity is *God manifesting*. Recall what we said above about God as the Ground of Being. Well, as Tillich defines it in his highly specialized language, the Word is "the principle of the divine self-manifestation in the ground of being itself." The ground of being has the character of self-manifestation; that's its *logos* character. The Ground is not only an abyss in which every form disappears; the Ground also is *the source* from which every form emerges. Second, the Word is the medium of creation, a dynamic spiritual word that functions as the mediator between "the silent mystery of the abyss of being and the fullness of concrete, individualized, self-related beings." And third, the Word is the manifestation of the divine life *in the history of revelation*. It is "the Word received by all those who are in a revelatory correlation." In other words, God speaks to those who are in relationship with God. And this makes history important because history now becomes salvation history, what the Divine uses to work out a plan in the fullness of time.

But back to the first meaning again: "The many different meanings of the term 'Word' are all united in one meaning, namely, 'God manifest' "—manifest in creation, manifest in the history of revelation, as well as manifest in the Bible and in the words of the church and its members. " 'God manifest'—the mystery of the divine abyss expressing itself through the divine Logos—this is the meaning of the symbol, the 'Word of God.' "[10]

It is a beautiful thing that our Muslim siblings refer to the common ground that we Jews and Christians share with them, that we are all *ahl al-Kitab*–the People of the Book. Many Protestant traditions, following the doctrine of *sola scriptura*, would be pleased with such a designation (especially if it only referred to the Bible). But are we People of the Word? In the fullest extent of what that "Word" contains?

We are still at the level here of the Word before words, the *logos* before logic as well as "the mediator to thinking that is not (yet?) thinking" and the "awareness that is not (yet?) understanding." The Second Person of the Trinity is first and foremost simply God manifesting.

DABHAR: *ACTION AND EVENT*

Once again we are going to start our rearticulating of the Second Person of the Trinity—which Bruno calls "the Word" and Panikkar refers to as the personalist dimension of the universal spiritual journey—by discovering the mountain underneath the island in the Hebrew scriptures.

In the Bible, at first we see the Word of God appear not quite as a person, but as *dabhar*, a Hebrew term that primarily means "word" or "talk" but also has the connotation of an event or a happening. Some will translate it as the creative energy of God. That is the word that gets translated into Greek as either *rhema* ("an utterance, a thing said") or more often as the famous *logos*. This is Tillich's second meaning, a dynamic spiritual word that is the medium of creation. We could associate *dabhar* with *action*. At the beginning of the Book of Genesis in the story of creation, for example, God speaks—what the Kabbalah tradition calls "the

---

[10]Tillich, *Systematic Theology*, vol. 1, 157–158.

ten utterances," *Yehi!* "Let there be . . ." —and things appear and are created. As Psalm 33 says:

> By God's word the heavens were made,
> By the breath of his mouth all the stars . . .
> For God spoke; it came to be.
> God commanded: it sprang into being.[11]

The mystical tradition of Judaism loves to meditate on numbers and letters and their inner significance. One theory among philologists concerning the etymology of the word *dabhar* points out that the same root consonants in *dabhar* (D-B-R) appear in the word for the innermost part of the Holy of Holies in Solomon's Temple–*debir* (as well as in the word for desert—*midbhar*). The Holy of Holies of course is where the Ark of the Covenant was kept, the book of the Law. And so, we could speculate on a connection between those things, the temple and word/action. Perhaps what binds these two terms together is the basic meaning of *dbr* as the preposition "behind," as in the divine presence and action *behind* the Temple veil, the divine presence and action *behind* the word. Saint Jerome translated *debir* as *oraculum*, "oracle," the temple as the place where the people listen to God and God listens to the people. God is *behind* the word and at any moment God's presence and action could break through the shell of the word, from behind the veil of the Temple. Wherever God's word is, God is present and acting.[12]

Let's say that's the masculine aspect of the Second Person of the Trinity, "God-in-action." But before we let *dabhar–logos*-Word, the masculine aspect, get the upper hand or the final word (again?), what is equally if not more important, as we shall see, is something

---

[11]Ps. 33:6, 9 (Grail).

[12]Father Chrysogonus Waddell, "Are There Lessons for Today in Twelfth-Century Sacred Music?" *Adoremus*, online edition, 12, no. 8 (November 2006). See also Damasus Winzen, *Pathways to Scripture*, quoted in *The Word in Season*, vol. 5, Saturday, Sixteenth Week in Ordinary Time (Villanova, PA: Augustinian Press, 1995), 224.

that, or Someone who, has been brought into higher relief for us by recent scholarship—Wisdom.

WISDOM

Wisdom can have a number of different meanings in scripture. It can simply be a literary genre, "the books of wisdom" such as Job, Ecclesiastes, and the Greek Deuterocanonical books Sirach and the Wisdom of Solomon. It can also refer to collections of the sayings of sages, "sayings of the wise," aphorisms that provide practical advice for living in an ethical and righteous way. The Book of Proverbs is the best example of this. We see this type of literature in other traditions as well: the Yoga Sutras of Patanjali, the early Buddhist monastic teaching known as the *Dhammapada*, the Tibetan classic *The Bodhisattva's Way of Life*.

But it's the third meaning of wisdom that is the foundational one for us: Wisdom as a *person*, invariably depicted in the Jewish wisdom literature in female form. She goes by a few different names. There is *chokmah* in Hebrew and *sapientia* later in Latin, both of which are feminine nouns. But most feminist theologians and scripture scholars prefer to use the word and the name *Sophia* for her, as she is known in the books of Wisdom and Sirach, which were written in Greek. The term "sophia" is used in the New Testament as well, such as when Paul refers to Jesus as "the *sophia* of God" (1 Cor. 1:24). As a matter of fact, many of these same scripture scholars will use the name Sophia even when referring to Lady Wisdom in the books that were originally written in Hebrew, precisely because Sophia is also a name and so conveys a female personification more than the word wisdom does.[13]

In Jewish literature, "Wisdom" is portrayed much more as a person than as an attribute of God. As the Carmelite scholar

---

[13]Marcus J. Borg, *Meeting Jesus Again for the First Time: The Historical Jesus and the Heart of Contemporary Faith* (New York: HarperOne, 1995), 98.

Constance Fitzgerald puts it, "Biblical wisdom is treated, not as
an it, but as a summoning 'I.' " She is a sister, a mother, a spouse,
a female beloved, a teacher, a chef, and a hostess.[14] My point here
is that it is not *dhabar* that is personified in scripture; *dhabar* is
more of an energy and an action than a person. It's the feminine
wisdom, Sophia, who is spoken of as relational, as a person.

There are those who think that the development and depiction of
the feminine figure of Wisdom in the Jewish scriptures may actually
have been influenced by one or more female deities outside of the
Bible, coming from one of the neighboring cultures with whom
the Hebrew culture rubbed elbows. The personification of Wisdom
might have been influenced by the Canaanite form of Astarte, and
of course here we are in the Holy Land itself (Canaan). Perhaps it
was influenced by the Mesopotamian goddess Ishtar. This would
be from the area known as the Fertile Crescent of the Tigris and
Euphrates, stretching all the way from Turkey down to Kuwait,
and especially Iran and Iraq, the homeland of Abraham. There is
evidence of the influence of the Egyptian Ma'at, who represented
justice, law and order at times personified as a female deity. Even
more believe, and there is evidence for this, that the Jewish notion
of Sophia was influenced by the Egyptian goddess Isis, who was
worshipped for over three thousand years, from about 3000 BCE
until well into the time of the Roman Empire. Isis took on many
different roles, and the titles and names of different goddesses, but
mainly she was worshipped as "the One who brings the many into
being, the feminine aspect of the primeval abyss from which all
life came."[15] That idea has some resonance with what we spoke of
earlier: the abyss of Being becomes the Great Mother, the "womb
of possibility."

The suggestion is that Judaism began personifying Wisdom

---

[14]Constance Fitzgerald, "Transformation in Wisdom: the Subversive Character
and Educative Power of Sophia in Contemplation," in *Carmel and Contemplation*,
ed. Kevin Culligan (Washington, DC: ICS Publications, 2000), 283.

[15]Andrew Harvey and Anne Baring, *The Divine Feminine: Exploring the Feminine
Face of God throughout the World* (Berkeley, CA: Conari Press, 1996), 42.

as female in these environments as a way of dealing with the threat that was posed by the cult of Isis, for instance, to ward off a temptation to doubt or be lured away from traditional faith. Ironically, when Christianity came to Egypt, many of Isis's shrines were rededicated to the Virgin Mary (who in the Litany of Loreto is called "Mary Seat of Wisdom").

It's important to point out that Judaism is still fiercely loyal to monotheism. There is no evidence that the biblical writers thought of themselves as introducing a second god into the tradition by introducing a female personification of Wisdom, and there was never any alternative cult of Sophia.[16] This has always been my hesitancy about even referring to the "Divine feminine," even though it took me a long time to figure out what was bothering me. "God the Mother," for instance, as I wrote earlier, always felt like next to God the Father (an old man with a white beard sitting on a throne). I now had God as Mother, an old woman sitting next to "Him," and that felt like no improvement, just another image/idol I had to get past.

In the Jewish scriptures we're almost speaking more of an androgynous image: God who is both mother and father, not two different Gods but Sophia as the feminine aspect of the divine. Sophia is so closely associated with God that sometimes she becomes indistinguishable from God in terms of her functions and the qualities that get ascribed to her. We could go so far as to say that Sophia "is not simply a personification of *wisdom* in female form"—as if Wisdom were another deity next to God—but "a personification of *God* in female form. Sophia is a female image of God, a lens through which divine reality [can be] imaged as a woman."[17]

So the Jews don't sacrifice their belief in monotheism; they simply bring forward "a feminine metaphor for the Divine that

---

[16]Denis Edwards, *Jesus the Wisdom of God: An Ecological Theology* (Eugene, OR: Wipf & Stock, 2005), 32.

[17]Borg, *Meeting Jesus Again for the First Time*, 102. Emphases mine.

was important for their age, and used it to speak about the God of Israel."[18] The dilemma of this is solved in a new and different way by our understanding of the Persons of the Trinity. Jews would never speak of Lady Wisdom as a separate Person; we Christians, however, would—and do. Remember we are speaking here of the Second Person, whom we either think of as "the Word" or identify exclusively with Jesus Christ. The Christian idea of the Persons in the Trinity is a way of explaining or describing this relationship of God to Sophia. Back to my old naïve question: Who was the Second Person of the Trinity before Jesus was born? What you see I am suggesting is that the Second Person of the Trinity is first introduced to us as Sophia, Wisdom as the preexistent Christ before Jesus was born.

And we return once again to Panikkar's notion of person as implying relationship: what we always note about Lady Wisdom are at least these three things, as we shall see in the canticles that we will look at below. First of all, she is always involved in creation, like Psalm 33 above. The Australian theologian Denis Edwards makes a big point of this and builds a whole ecological theology around it—*Jesus the Wisdom of God: An Ecological Theology*. Second, she is always relational. And third—and this may be the most important aspect—she particularly *delights to be with the human race*; she particularly delights in being in relationship with human beings.

The First Person, the Silence, speaks; Being manifests; the Great Mother gives birth, because although the unnamable is the origin of heaven and earth, when it is named, it is the mother of the ten thousand things.

---

[18]Fitzgerald, "Transformation in Wisdom," in *Carmelite Studies*, 282.

6

Wisdom Builds Her House

There are four canticles in three books of the Jewish scriptures where Wisdom makes her appearance, Proverbs, Sirach, and the Wisdom of Solomon. Though she also shows up in Job and the prophet Baruch, it is Proverbs, Sirach, and the Wisdom of Solomon that get mentioned over and over by scripture scholars as where Wisdom appears, speaks, and acts as a fully developed personal being: an attractive, mysterious, powerful, and relational woman.

These canticles had a profound influence on the writings of John of the Cross. There is also an early anonymous but influential Franciscan text known as "The Sacred Exchange between Saint Francis and Lady Poverty," written to encourage Francis's followers to continue in the line of the saint's biblical vision of poverty, with Lady Poverty as the personification of biblical Wisdom and an image of the Church for Francis's life and charism.

PROVERBS 8–9: BELOVED CHILD AND ARTISAN

The first canticle we will examine is found in Proverbs 8. There are several places where *chokmah*, or "wisdom" in biblical Hebrew, makes an appearance in Proverbs, but we will confine ourselves to the two canticles where she is clearly Lady Wisdom.[1]

The canticle begins, "The Lord created me at the beginning of his work" (v. 22). Australian theologian Denis Edwards then walks us through three important theological insights about Wisdom in what follows. First, God begot or created her as the firstborn, "the first of his acts of long ago" (v. 22). This image will morph somewhat in other Wisdom canticles, where her appearance is described more as emanating rather than begotten. She was created before all natural things, older than the oldest things known, "when there were no depths, no springs abounding with water, before the mountains had been shaped, before the hills, when he had not yet made earth and fields" (vv. 24–25).

Second, not only is she described as God's child; Wisdom is also God's companion, with God from the beginning: "When he established the heavens, I was there" (v. 27); and God's co-worker, participating, cooperating with God in creation

> . . . when he drew a circle on the face of the deep,
> when he made firm the skies above,
> when he established the fountains of the deep,
> when he assigned to the sea its limit,
> so that the waters might not transgress his command,
> when he marked out the foundations of the earth. . . .
>   (vv. 27–29)

Verse 30 then says, "then I was beside him, like a master worker."

So, is Wisdom a favorite child or a skilled worker? Perhaps it's deliberately ambiguous, almost as if the author is throwing out a variety of images to describe this relationship between her and God. Either way, it is through Wisdom that God created the world; Wisdom is the chief artisan who executed the divine plan. Keep in mind that we are seeing here the first glimmers of the Second Person of the Trinity—as a *person*.

---

[1]See the Appendix.

Third, Wisdom delights in creation, "rejoicing in his inhabited world" and particularly "delighting in the human race" (v. 31). Here we see that Wisdom is profoundly relational—not only interrelated with God, but also interrelated with all creatures and with humans in a special way. In fact, as we see in the following canticle from chapter 9, she wants to throw them a big banquet—of bread and wine, which ought to sound familiar to Christians:

> Wisdom has built her house,
> she has hewn her seven pillars.
> She has slaughtered her animals,
> she has mixed her wine,
> she has also set her table. . . .
> To those without sense she says,
> "Come, eat of my bread
> and drink of the wine I have mixed. (vv. 1–2, 4–5)

We could add here one more trait: Wisdom is also the divine summons, since "she has sent out her servant-girls and calls from the highest places in the town: 'You that are simple, turn in here!'" (v. 3).

This image is going to influence the whole subsequent Wisdom tradition, particularly among the Hellenized (Greek-speaking) Jewish diaspora in Alexandria the last three hundred years before the Christian era. And, looking ahead, we can already catch a glimpse of how this "will give shape to Jesus' ministry in his meals and parables, and to the interpretation of his ministry."[2]

This personification of Wisdom and the attribution to her of divine qualities is even more developed in the Deuterocanonical books, sometimes called the "intertestamental" books, because they stand between the Old and the New Testaments. These are books from Alexandrian Judaism that were received and accepted by the early church as part of the Greek version of the Jewish scriptures.

---

[2]Denis Edwards, *Jesus the Wisdom of God: An Ecological Theology* (Eugene, OR: Wipf & Stock, 2005), 23–24.

Though popular with the early Christians, they were not included in the non-Greek Jewish Hebrew version of the Bible and were also later rejected by the Protestant tradition. Since they are written in Greek, we will now have the word/name *Sophia* instead of *Chokmah.*

SIRACH 24: TRAVELING WISDOM

Next we turn to two canticles in Sirach and Wisdom (or the Wisdom of Solomon). Sirach comes from the Hellenistic era, the three hundred years before Christ when the tradition of Jewish wisdom developed and reached its peak. We learn at the end of Sirach chapter 50 that the book was written by "Jesus son of Eleazar son of Sirach of Jerusalem" (v. 27). But as we find out in the preface, it had then been translated into Greek from the Hebrew by his grandson for the Jewish community in Alexandria.

Sirach also gives us the one known date we have for this Wisdom period of Jewish scripture: the grandson arrived in Egypt "in the thirty-eighth year of the reign of Euergetes" (prologue), around 132 years before the Common Era. Here too, like the temptation to go over to the cult of Isis, it appears that the author or the translator is resisting the pressure to conform to Greek ways. As the grandson tells us,

> My grandfather Jesus, who had devoted himself especially to the reading of the Law and the Prophets, . . . was himself also led to write something pertaining to instruction and wisdom, so that by becoming familiar also with his book those who love learning might make even greater progress in living according to the law. (Prologue to the book of Sirach)

Jesus ben Sira is not against accepting what is good in the Greek culture—*sophia*-wisdom, learning—but he is arguing that one can find true Wisdom only in relationship with the God of Israel.

With the very first verse he states his case: "All wisdom is from the Lord, and with him it remains for ever" (1:1).

Sophia-Wisdom appears in three major places in the book, but it is especially the canticle in chapter 24 that stands out for its beauty and strength—her central speech in the assembly of the Most High, in the heavenly court, proclaiming her divine origin: "Wisdom praises herself, and tells of her glory in the midst of her people" (24:1). She then claims that she has come "forth from the mouth of the Most High" (v. 3). Remember this phrase. "Before the ages, in the beginning, he created me, and for all the ages I shall not cease to be" (v. 9). She "covered the earth like mist" (v. 3), as the breath of God covers the earth. Note here the resonances with the creation story. She "compassed the vault of heaven" and has "traversed the depths of the abyss. Over waves of the sea, over all the earth" (vv. 5–6). Roland Murphy asks, "Is this really God in the figure of travelling Wisdom?"[3] Again, more a personification of God than a separate deity. She held sway "over every people and nation" (v. 6) looking for a resting place, but she ultimately found a permanent home in Israel, because "my Creator chose the place for my tent. He said, 'Make your dwelling in Jacob, and in Israel receive your inheritance'" (v. 8).

And from here she again issues an invitation to a great banquet, but now it is she herself who is the food and drink, the source of nourishment and life, which again ought to sound familiar to followers of Jesus.

> Come to me, you who desire me,
> and eat your fill of my fruits.
> For the memory of me is sweeter than honey,
> and the possession of me sweeter than the honeycomb.
> Those who eat of me will hunger for more,
> and those who drink of me will thirst for more.
>   (vv. 19–21)

---

[3]Roland Murphy, *The Tree of Life: An Exploration of Biblical Wisdom* (New York: Doubleday, 1990), 137.

For Sirach, Wisdom is Torah, and Torah is food. This may be the most radical innovation and original idea of Sirach, identifying Wisdom with Torah with all that that entails, the tradition, history, and laws of Israel. Later we will see this image of nourishment echoed in the Christian scriptures, particularly in the bread of life discourse in the Gospel of John. This is also an important inheritance for the Christian understanding of the connection between the Eucharist and the Word—as Jesus himself quotes Deuteronomy 8:3 in his temptation in the desert: "'One does not live by bread alone, but by every word that comes from the mouth of the Lord'" (Mt. 4:4; Lk. 4:4).

WISDOM 7: EFFUSION AND EMANATION

The Wisdom of Solomon is written in the name of King Solomon, but it seems to have been written very close to the Christian era, perhaps even during Jesus' lifetime, also presumably by a Hellenized Jew, probably from Alexandria again. What's interesting about the attribution and association with Solomon is that Solomon seems to have had a real propensity both for Wisdom and for the feminine in general, given his many wives and especially his fabled relationship with the Queen of Sheba. Recall the goddess Astarte whom we mentioned earlier? In 1 Kings we find out that

> when Solomon was old, his wives turned away his heart after other gods; and his heart was not true to the Lord his God, as was the heart of his father David. For Solomon followed Astarte the goddess of the Sidonians, and Milcom the abomination of the Ammonites.[4]

---

[4]1 Kgs. 1:4–5. Milcom was the national god of the Ammonites, one of the foreign gods for whom Solomon built a high place on the Mount of Olives (1 Kgs. 11:5, 7, 33). This was later destroyed by Josiah (2 Kgs. 23:13).

My own speculation—not to excuse his idolatry or worship of other gods, but I wonder if there isn't something in the prophetic traditions in general that longs to fill this purely masculine imagery out a little, longing for a female aspect of the Divine. And so Wisdom, Sophia, becomes Solomon's beloved.

There is a beautiful story recorded twice, once in First Kings and then again in Chronicles, when God appears to Solomon and asks him what he wants as a gift. Solomon, instead of asking for possessions, wealth, honor, or the life of those who hate him, or even for long life, asks for "wisdom and knowledge to go out and come in before this people, for who can rule this great people of yours?" This pleases God, who then grants him wisdom in addition to "riches, possessions, and honor, such as none of the kings had who were before you, and none after you shall have the like" (2 Chron. 1:7–12).

Though the Book of Wisdom is intensely Jewish, it is thoroughly stamped with Greek thought, another reason why this Hellenized Judaism is an important bridge between the two Testaments. This is one of the examples of Hebrew mythological language meeting Greek philosophy; because Jewish thought does not have its own metaphysics, its own philosophical language, it had to "borrow" one. (There are those who would argue it would have been better to stay with the symbolic mythic and poetic language!) However, this is one of the arguments that others make to emphasize that the marriage of Hebrew thought and Greek thought was providential.

In the second section of the book, between chapters 6 and 11, there appears a great celebration of divine Wisdom and also a description of Solomon's love affair with her—"I loved her [Wisdom] more than health or beauty" (7:10). The author says that he was led to Sophia through the various sciences, the study of the stars, plants, and animals, even chemicals, and the study of the human mind and behavior—all wisdom that comes from Sophia because she is the *technitis*,[5] the artisan of all this, at work in creation.

---

[5]Wis. 7:22, 8:6.

Then comes this amazing hymn in chapter 7, singing all her twenty-one attributes (a perfect number—seven multiplied by three).

> There is in her a spirit that is
> intelligent, holy, unique, manifold,
> subtle, mobile, clear, unpolluted,
> distinct, invulnerable, loving the good,
> keen, irresistible, beneficent, humane,
> steadfast, sure, free from anxiety,
> all-powerful, overseeing all,
> and penetrating through all spirits
> that are intelligent, pure, and altogether subtle. (7:22–23)

Here she is a sort of radiation from the divinity: "more mobile than any motion; because of her pureness she pervades and penetrates all things. For she is a breath of the power of God, and a pure emanation of the glory of the Almighty." We see a similarity with the hymn at the beginning of the Letter to the Hebrews when the author says that the Son, "whom God appointed heir of all things, through whom he also created the worlds, is also the reflection of God's glory and the exact imprint of God's very being, and he sustains all things by his powerful word" (Heb. 1:3).

Wisdom is God's presence to the universe in continuous creation: "while remaining in herself, she renews all things" (7:27). And in verses 11–12 of the same chapter we learn that she is the mother of all good things, and in verse 21 she is their fashioner. Is this the Second Person of the Trinity as mother?

She is the Divine mind immanent within the universe, guiding and controlling all its dynamic operations, "a reflection of eternal light, a spotless mirror of the working of God, and an image of his goodness" (7:26). In the next chapter we are told that "she glorifies her noble birth by living with God" (8:3). A very strong word in Greek is used—*symbiōsis*, "the same life," which might remind us of the Greek word *homoousios*, "consubstantial," nuancing any idea of a separate deity. Two chapters later, in chapter 10, Sophia is presented as a Savior! All the saving deeds of God are attributed to her: "A holy people and blameless race wisdom delivered from a nation of oppressors. . . . She brought them over the Red Sea, and led them through deep waters; but she drowned their enemies, and cast them up from the depths of the sea" (Wis. 10:15, 18–19).

Kathleen O'Connor says that now we see that Sophia is God, "not a new god, or a second god, but God poetically imaged as a woman."[6] I would accent that this is a clear glimpse of the Second Person of the Trinity as a person.

We cannot end this section without quoting the end of the canticle in chapter 7.

> She is more beautiful than the sun,
> and excels every constellation of the stars.
> Compared with the light she is found to be superior,
> for it is succeeded by the night,
> but against wisdom evil does not prevail. (vv. 29–30)

Then it ends with another phrase to remember well: "She reaches mightily from one end of the earth to the other, and she orders all things well" (8:1).

THE JESUS MOVEMENT: SOPHIA BECOMES LOGOS

In the earliest days of the Jesus movement the great theological and Christological definitions had not yet solidified into what we know and have known rather exclusively at least since the time of the Council of Nicaea in 325 CE—namely, the "only begotten Son of the Father," which, by the way, I am not contesting or challeng-

---

[6]Kathleen M. O'Connor, *The Wisdom Literature* (Collegeville, MN: Liturgical Press, 1990), 178.

ing at all. What others have suggested, though, is that this is not the *only* way to describe the relationship of the Second Person of the Trinity to the First Person, nor was it always the main way in the earliest days of the Jesus movement, especially when speaking about the preexistent Christ, the Second Person of the Trinity before Jesus was born. And we can see hints of other christologies in the scriptures and the ancient writings of Christianity.

One of the other early theological approaches to an understanding of Jesus, of which we see copious mentions in the Christian scriptures, if you know what you are looking for, was through identifying Jesus with Divine Wisdom.[7] Is Jesus *dabhar* made flesh? Sure. Is Jesus *chokmah*–Sophia/Wisdom made flesh? Absolutely.

There are also little hints hidden all over the liturgical tradition. One of the strongest happens during the seven days before Christmas. At evening prayers, Vespers, as usual the Canticle of Mary (the Magnificat) is sung or recited, and as usual it is introduced by an antiphon. However, what is unique on these days is a 1,500-year-old tradition, that each of the antiphons for these days begins with the vocative "O," in the original Latin and in most translations. These "O Antiphons" each invoke a title of the Christ we are waiting for. Most people will know the famous traditional hymn, "O Come, O Come Emmanuel." That is actually the last of the O antiphons, and the other verses of the song are based on the other six, "O come, O Key of David, O Root of Jesse, O Dayspring," and so on. But the very first O antiphon, on December 17, is *O Sapientia, quae ex ore Altissimi prodiisti, attingens a fine usque ad finem*: "O Wisdom who came out of the mouth of the Most High, reaching from end to end and ordering all things mightily and sweetly." Do you recognize that? That antiphon is drawn directly from the Greek Sophia canticles we looked at, Sirach 24:5: "I came forth from the mouth of the Most High," and Wisdom 8:1: "She reaches mightily from one end of the earth to the other, and she orders all things well."

---

[7]Edwards, *Jesus the Wisdom of God*, 19.

The very first name we use to call this Second Person of the Trinity about to be made flesh in Jesus is *Sapientia*, Sophia, Lady Wisdom. Someone around the sixth or seventh century was dropping crumbs on the path, lest we forget Sophia completely.

Another large hint is architectural, the great church of Hagia Sophia in Constantinople, the church of "Holy Wisdom," which is said to be dedicated to the Second Person of the Trinity, whose patronal feast falls on December 25, the commemoration of the incarnation of the Logos in Christ. But it's not called *Hagia Logos*, the Holy Word; it's called *Hagia Sophia*, the church of Holy Wisdom.

The Christian tradition will claim that Jesus is Word-Made-Flesh. It is one important step to realize and appreciate that the Second Person of the Trinity is primarily the Word, even before being born as Jesus. Now we see more of the mountain beneath the island in realizing that it is just as appropriate, perhaps even *more* appropriate, to say that the Second Person of the Trinity is Wisdom and that the preexistent Christ is Sophia. How does she come to be eclipsed by Logos and, more important, how might we come to see her in all her beauty again? Before we answer that, let's explore what Greek philosophy means by *logos*—"word"—and how it slips into the Christian tradition.

THE GREEK LOGOS

There are many religious and philosophical systems that have a notion of a great intelligence principle behind the cosmos, the divine intentionality of the universe. I want to mention two: the Taoist philosophy of China and, especially for our purposes, this *logos* of Greek philosophy, which we inherit directly into Christianity. First, the Greek.

The best earliest example is from the Greek philosopher Heraclitus.[8] He was called "the Obscure" because he often spoke and

---

[8] Pre-Socratic Ionian philosopher, c. 535–c. 475 BCE.

taught in riddles. Heraclitus based his whole philosophy on the notion of there being a divine universal reason, which he called the Logos, that was the structure or pattern of the world, a pattern, mind you, that is only revealed to the contemplative gaze, concealed from the eyes of ordinary people. Heraclitus was almost a Buddhist in that his chief idea was that everything is in flux. (He's the one credited with the aphorism, "You cannot step in the same river twice," which for years I actually thought was a Taoist saying!). And yet he argued that, despite this constant flux, there must be some basic unity underlying these many forms. That's the Logos: the unity that lies beneath the surface, the unity of conflicting opposites. Amid all this change it is the Logos that maintains a continual balance, a kind of ground.[9]

Then there were the Stoics, a school of philosophy that stretched from Zeno in the fourth century BCE through Cicero up to Marcus Aurelius.[10] Heraclitus influenced the Stoics, and the Stoics in turn influenced not only St. Paul, with whom they debated in Acts 17 earlier, but also Clement of Alexandria and Origen. The Stoics were predominant in the first century BCE. Their notion of *logos* is very attractive. Logos is the mind of God (though a pantheistic God), and all things and all people are under its control as it unifies the whole structure of matter like a force, a fiery substance that permeates everything, "guiding, controlling, and directing all things."[11] A passage in Marcus Aurelius's *Meditations* tells us that "Nature is pliant, obedient. And the *logos* that governs it . . . dictates all beginnings and endings."[12] We could see all three Persons of the Trinity in this: the mind (the Second Person) of God (the First Person) is a fiery force, an energy (the Third Person).

---

[9]This differentiates Heraclitus from Buddhist thought; the Buddha would say there is no unifying ground, only *anika*—impermanence and dependent co-arising.

[10]106–43 BCE and 121–180 CE respectively.

[11]Raymond Brown, *The Gospel According to John (i–xxii)* (Garden City, NY: Doubleday, 1966), 520.

[12]Marcus Aurelius, *Meditations: Living, Dying and the Good Life*, trans. Gregory Hays (London: Weidenfeld & Nicholson, 2003), 77.

It's also instructive to recall exactly what this philosophical concept *logos*-"word" had come to mean to Jesus' Jewish contemporaries, especially the Greek-speaking Jews. Again, this Alexandrian Greek influence on Jewish thought cannot be underestimated for its influence. This little point is very important: the Hellenistic Alexandrians would tend to see the *logos* as a sort of mediator between the Divine and the created. The best example is Philo, a Hellenized Jewish philosopher who lived from 20 BC to 50 AD and so is a contemporary of Jesus. He was one of the first to popularize the term among the Jews; he used the word over 1,200 times in his works. For Philo, the logos was both divine wisdom and the creative principle, and, like the Greeks, he also thought that it was necessary to maintain the distinction between the perfect idea (God) and imperfect matter. And that's why the logos was necessary, he taught: because God cannot come into contact with matter, which would also coincide with Greek philosophy. As Sarah Ruden explains, Philo could apply this kind of dualism "in the name of cosmopolitan assimilation."[13] Philo's logos is "neither divine nor created, but midway between the two." Philo's logos is not God, but to link the divine and the created he wanted *logos* to be something more than a creature.[14]

THE TAO

Now a word about the *Tao te Ching*, which I have brought into the conversation several times already.

The *Tao te Ching* is a book of mysticism and philosophy of incredible depth and at the same time utter simplicity that had an enormous impact on all subsequent Chinese culture, particularly Chinese herbal medicine and what is sometimes called "Chinese yoga"—breathing exercises and meditation practices, as well as

---

[13]Sarah Ruden, "Origins and Scriptures," *National Review*, October 30, 2017, 45.
[14]Louis Bouyer, *The Fourth Gospel* (Grand Rapids, MI: Eerdmans, 1983), 34.

martial arts. When Buddhism comes out of India and into China, it meets Taoism and takes on a new form and expression, what we know as the Zen tradition. So Taoism also serves as a bridge between Indian thought and subsequent Asian Buddhist thought. The *Tao te Ching* comes from what is known as the First Axial Period, sometime around 500 years before the Common Era, and its legendary author is Lao Tzu. It is not quite clear if Lao Tzu was a real historical personage, but there are some tales of him in conversation with the great Confucius.

Why this school of thought is important (and why it became very important to me) is that many people have written convincingly that the Chinese concept of the *tao* is very much what the Greek concept of *logos* is also trying to convey, the *tao* or the *logos* as that subtle intelligent principle of the universe, its intelligent design, you might say. Further, with all due respect for the Greek tradition, the *Tao te Ching* is considered by many to be the most sublime teaching about this concept.

Lao Tzu, like Heraclitus, repeatedly states that the tao can't be named, can't be understood: "The Tao that can be named is not the eternal Tao" is how the whole book gets started. But this is where the *Tao te Ching* shines in a way that Greek thought does not: this apophatic mystical element remains a central concept throughout the work—the "awareness that is not (yet?) understanding." And, according to Lao Tzu, this intelligent principle, this *logos* or *tao*, is not a big flashy thing. It's not a monstrosity of a structure or a great super-imposing force. As the *Tao te Ching*, chapter 8, says, the *tao* is more like water: "nurturing the ten thousand things without competing, flowing into places people scorn." Here again we have the idea of a pervading presence. For example, chapter 34 says that

The great *tao* is all-pervading.
It reaches to the left and to the right.
All things depend on it with their existence.
Still, it demands no obedience.

JOHANNINE LOGOS

When we turn to Christianity, we are dealing mainly with the Gospel of John, which is the only New Testament gospel that explicitly brings *dabhar-chokmah/sophia* into Christology, the Christian understanding of who Jesus is. When the Gospel of John was written, the author most likely didn't know the *Tao te Ching*, but undoubtedly knew this Greek concept of *logos*. But the Gospel of John doesn't just borrow *logos*, but transforms it when it asserts that not only was the Word with God, but that the Word *was* God and that this God/Word became flesh—and "we have seen his glory" (Jn. 1:14).

We are speaking specifically about the prologue of his gospel, John's hymn to the Word:

> In the beginning was the Word-*Logos*,
> and the Word was with God,
> and the Word was God.
> He was in the beginning with God.
> All things came into being through him,
> and without him not one thing came into being.
> What has come into being in him was life,
> and the life was the light of all people.
> The light shines in the darkness,
> and the darkness did not overcome it. . . .
> And the Word became flesh and lived among us,
> and we have seen his glory,
> the glory as of a father's only son,
> full of grace and truth. (Jn. 1:1–5, 14)

Incidentally, as further proof that the Chinese understanding of the tao is equivalent to the Greek logos, when the Gospel of John is translated into Chinese most translations render it:

In the beginning was the *Tao*,
and the *Tao* was with God,
and the *Tao* was God.
Tao was in the beginning with God.
All things came into being through *Tao*,
and without *Tao* not one thing came into being. . . .
And the *Tao* became flesh and lived among us.[15]

Since the Tao is also known as the Great Mother, perhaps instead of saying that tao is a good substitute for logos, it would be better to say that Tao is even more an equivalent of Sophia.

Something mysteriously formed,
Born before heaven and earth.
In the silence and the void,
Standing alone and unchanging,
Ever present and in motion.
Perhaps it is the mother of ten thousand things.
I do not know its name.
Call it *Tao*.
For lack of a better word, I call it great. (#25)

And look at this, in relation to the prologue of the Gospel of John:

In the beginning was the *Tao*.
All things issue from it;
all things return to it.

To find the origin,
trace back the manifestations.
When you recognize the children

---

[15]Biblical Hermeneutics, https://hermeneutics.stackexchange.com/questions/2307/why-do-many-chinese-bibles-translate-logos-in-john-11-as-%E9%81%93-dao. See, for instance, Good News Translation, Today's Chinese Translation (Swindon, UK: United Bible Societies, 2015).

and find the mother,
you will be free of sorrow. (#52)

So here again we have evidence of another tradition that could possibly teach us something about our own tradition, another way of expressing the same truth: to see Jesus as *Tao*-Made-Flesh and perhaps learn some nuance about this Second Person of the Trinity from the Chinese tradition instead of or in addition to *Logos* and *Sophia*. I find this especially poignant given that, besides the mystical silent aspect of the Second Person, the tao also carries in it the yin-yang, feminine-masculine complementarity of logos-sophia in a way that logos by itself does not. The feminine-masculine means more than genders too. It's a philosophical concept at the very heart of Chinese thought and culture, spiritual practice and medicine. Among its other multivalent meanings, it is also the meeting of heaven and earth, which are mentioned together often in the *Tao te Ching* and other Taoist writings: chapter 32, for example, sings that "Heaven and earth come together in harmony and sweet rain falls everywhere."[16] That meeting of heaven and earth ought to be of particular interest to those who believe that the Word was made flesh.

Remember that for Philo and the Greeks (as well as the Gnostics), God cannot come into contact with matter. "God cannot come down to the level of humanity. . . . Philo's *logos* cannot be incarnate."[17] So what a scandal it would have been for the evangelist to say that the *Logos* is not just a mediator, but that the *Logos* was with God, and the *Logos* was God! This is the specifically Christian view that is different from that of anyone else—that the Word was made flesh. Augustine claimed that he found everything else in Christianity in Greek philosophy, except this: no one ever spoke of Word-Made-Flesh. This will be orthodox Christianity's argu-

---

[16]Other examples: *Tao te Ching* #1 and #25 speak of the Tao as *something mysterious* that *existed before heaven and earth*; and #5 tells us that *heaven and earth are not sentimental*.

[17]Bouyer, *The Fourth Gospel*, 35.

ment against Gnosticism, taken up especially by Irenaeus of Lyons.

The prologue of John is a hymn, really, that got inserted at the beginning of John's narrative, and is generally thought to have been modeled on an older hymn or hymns to Wisdom, such as the one from the book of Sirach that we saw, in which Wisdom praises herself.

> Then the Creator of all things gave me a commandment
> and the one who had created me assigned a place for my
>   tent.
> and he said, "Make your dwelling in Jacob . . ."[18]

Some translations of the prologue echo the image from this Sirach hymn and render it "The Word of God became flesh and pitched a tent among us," an echo of the Jewish Feast of Tabernacles. A New Testament rendering of this might be "make your place not just in Jacob but make your place among and within human beings." As a matter of fact, Raymond Brown says that all three of the canticles that we looked at (from Proverbs, Sirach, and Wisdom) offer a parallel to John's hymn to the Word in their general literary form.[19] There are studies that go line for line to show this, which we won't go into here.

John's prologue hymn begins the same way the book of Genesis begins (as well as *Tao te Ching* #52): "In the beginning when God created the heavens and the earth" as compared to "In the beginning was the Word" (and "In the beginning was the *Tao*"). Remember how Wisdom is always associated with creation, so here is our first hint that this is Wisdom in John's thought.

There are some scholars who don't even want to translate the word *logos* from the Greek because it is so hard to convey what this concept meant to the Greek mind. Why that is unsatisfying, as

---

[18]Sir. 24:1*ff.* Note that this Sirach canticle is paired with the prologue of John on the 2nd Sunday after Christmas, a rarely used liturgy due to Epiphany being celebrated on a Sunday in most places now.

[19]Brown, *The Gospel According to John*, 522.

both Louis Bouyer and Raymond Brown insist, is because John is not using *logos* in the Greek sense of the word like Heraclitus, the Stoics, or Philo did. As a matter of fact, Bouyer says that to "claim that John depends on Greek thought is an absurdity"![20] John is doing something brand new.

So, the question remains: Is Jesus *dabhar–logos,* "God in action"- made flesh? Or is Jesus *chokmah/sophia*—the Person of Wisdom— who has now morphed into *logos*-made-flesh? Undoubtedly some of each, but there are those who would say that at least in the Gospel of John, Jesus is much more an incarnation of Wisdom. We can say with certainty—and this is backed up by scriptural scholars running the gamut—that the *logos* John is talking about "is *also* the Wisdom described by the psalmist and sage in Old Testament times, and . . . that Word and Wisdom alike became incarnate in Jesus."[21] Brown is even stronger, saying that in the Jewish presentation of Wisdom, "there are good parallels for almost every detail of the Prologue's description of the Word. The Prologue has carried personification [even] further than the Old Testament did in describing Wisdom," a development stemming, obviously, from the incarnation.[22]

The concept of divine wisdom, which had become more and more personified, is now joined here to the idea of God's creative word. "Divine, and yet almost distinct from God, wisdom had a role in creation; wisdom was sent forth from the mouth of God and helps save [humanity]." "We have a union of wisdom and God's word," as "a divine person uncreated and existing with the Father."[23] Here is the preexistent Christ the Second Person of the Trinity before Jesus was born—*Sophia, Tao, Logos.*

---

[20]Bouyer, *The Fourth Gospel,* 36.

[21]F. F. Bruce, *The Gospel of John: Introduction, Exposition and Notes* (Grand Rapids, MI: Eerdmans, 1983), 31–32. Emphasis mine.

[22]Brown, *The Gospel According to John,* 523.

[23]Raymond E. Brown, *The Gospel and Epistles of John: A Concise Commentary* (Collegeville, MN: Liturgical Press, 1988), 21–22.

7

Traces of Wisdom,
Seeds of the Word

So how or why did Sophia get replaced by Logos? Or how or why did Lady Wisdom get completely replaced by "only begotten son"? Of course, first of all, there is the gender of Jesus, and very soon the Second Person of the Trinity will be identified exclusively with Jesus the Christ, sometimes neglecting even a full understanding of the Second Person as the Word, let alone Wisdom.

Also, as noted earlier, Sophia had reached her peak of power as a divine person in the Jewish tradition during the Hellenistic era, the three hundred years before the birth of Jesus. And as we saw already with Philo, in that era there was the tendency to use the Greek term *logos* instead of Sophia. Jewish monotheism had already limited the possibility of Lady Wisdom growing into fully divine status because it did not have the language for nor an understanding of *perichoresis* as Christianity does, the mutual indwelling of persons. Nor did the first Christians either, by the way. It took a while for Christianity to come up with an adequate formulation to explain how there could be three persons and one God, and I dare say many Christians still do not understand it. Remember that neither the actual words nor the concepts of "nature" or of "person," which we have grown so dependent on in our understanding of the Trinity, are ever used in the New Testament in relationship to the Trinity. So the first generation of Christians lived out their faith without ever speaking of three "persons" in one God or two natures in one person.

Gnosticism held a place of influence in the time of early Christianity. Gnosticism favored Sophia, but it did her no favors in its association with her. Despite Gnosticism's perennial appeal (perhaps due to a misunderstanding of its philosophical underpinnings), it was dualistic, positing again an unbridgeable distance between the Creator and fallen creation. Gnosticism believed in an inferior deity called the Demiurge who had created the material universe, a position that Christian orthodoxy vehemently rejected. Another way in which Gnosticism was dualistic was that the Gnostics downplayed both the humanity (not the divinity) of Jesus and the crucifixion. Hence the crucifixion never appears in the so-called "gnostic gospels." The Jewish Sophia tradition had also never associated the personification of Wisdom/Sophia with suffering and dying, so that again made Christ-Sophia particularly attractive—no suffering. "These were not petty quarrels but fundamental disagreements about what life meant."[1]

Beyond that, Sophia perhaps fit in *too* well with the Gnostic understanding of Jesus, because she appears as a divine figure who came down from God with a special message. And that is somehow at the root of Gnosticism—a special message only for the initiated. The word "gnostic" comes from the Greek word *gnosis* or "knowledge." For the Gnostic it is special knowledge that saves—knowledge of Jesus' *message*—rather than the Paschal Mystery of Jesus' life, death, resurrection, ascension, and the sending of the Holy Spirit. If you just know the right thing, the right technique, the right language . . . We easily fall into various types of gnosticism in our own day and age.

All of this would urge orthodox Christianity to distance itself

---

[1]Susan Cole, Marian Ronan, and Hal Taussig, *Sophia: The Future of Feminist Spirituality* (San Francisco: Harper & Row, 1986), 51.

as far as possible from this image of Christ: the "proclamation of Jesus as Sophia was practically tantamount to accepting the gnostic stance against Jesus' humanity."[2] This could be the main reason that the New Testament gives only a muted acknowledgment of Lady Wisdom.

In addition to all that, it also seems beyond doubt that more than a little androcentrism played a big part in replacing Sophia with Logos. I mean that the Greco-European culture, and specifically the educated culture, was focused rather exclusively on men to the exclusion of women. Hence the decision, perhaps even unconscious, that a male term would be more suitable than this female figure. Feminist theologians often add that Sophia was finally pretty much completely erased as a part of the Christological tradition by the church fathers because of some outright misogyny in the patristic era.

Where Lady Wisdom will appear again, or at least some of her characteristics, is in the figure of the Holy Spirit, as we shall see. With the Holy Spirit there was not so much a danger of there being a heretical deviation in the early church. Seeing the Holy Spirit as feminine was a legitimate view that simply got marginalized instead of completely eclipsed, more so by Western Christianity than by Eastern Christianity.

SEEDS OF THE WORD

Sophia makes an appearance here too in a pithy little phrase, "seeds of the Word," in the writings of a second-century saint, Justin Martyr.

Justin was a philosopher who came to believe that Christianity was the true philosophy. There were two sides to his conversion. As he says while being led to his death before the Roman Consul Rusticus, he had tried to learn every system before he came to

---

[2]Ibid., 52.

believe that Christianity was the true philosophy. However, even though he had come to regard Christianity as the true philosophy, *he didn't dismiss the other philosophies out of hand.* He saw Plato and other pagan philosophers as not only pre-Christian but *pro-*Christian—other traditions too were/are pointing toward Christ. It is from him that we get the Christian use of the phrase *semina verbi* in Latin, or *spermatikos logos* in Greek—seeds of the Word. This was already a concept among Stoic philosophers. Justin thought that all those "who live in accordance with reason [*logos*] are Christians," even if they were godless. Here is a Christian saying that the Word (and Wisdom) can be detected outside the visible boundaries of Christianity. This predates the later famous phrase "anonymous Christian" by the twentieth-century theologian Karl Rahner, by about 1,700 years.

This is a concept near and dear to those of us who work in interreligious dialogue, though I must say there are narrow and broad interpretations of the concept. Some claim that Justin was referring only to Greek philosophers, and so it's not applicable to other so-called pagan religions and their philosophies. But Vatican II had a broader interpretation of the concept. The phrase *semina verbi* appears in both *Lumen Gentium* 17 and *Ad Gentes* 11, which apply it broadly, teaching that "seeds of the Word" were implanted in all human beings, and it is that which allows all people some ability to see spiritual realities, and so whatever is "true and holy" in other traditions can be upheld. John Paul II understood it this way as well:

> I have wished to recall the ancient doctrine formulated by the Fathers of the Church, which says that we must recognize "the seeds of the Word" present and active in the various religions.[3] This doctrine leads us to affirm that, though the routes taken may be different, "there is but a single goal to which is directed the deepest aspiration of the human spirit

---

[3]He cites both *Ad Gentes*, n. 11, and *Lumen Gentium,* n. 17, of Vatican II.

as expressed in its quest for God and also in its quest, through its tending towards God, *for the full dimension of its humanity*, or in other words, for the full meaning of human life." The "seeds of truth" present and active in the various religious traditions are a reflection of the unique Word of God, who "enlightens every [one] coming into the world" and who became flesh in Christ Jesus. They are together an "effect of the Spirit of truth operating outside the visible confines of the Mystical Body" and which "blows where it wills."[4]

Note this recognition, by a pope, that Lady Wisdom is operating even outside the visible confines of the Mystical Body simply in the aspiration for our full humanity.

Both Matthew and Luke record Jesus saying something rather remarkable concerning the Queen of Sheba (or the "queen of the South" as she is called in the gospels), who sought out Solomon because she recognized Solomon's wisdom.[5] The Qur'an mentions this story as well, although there she is referred to as *Bilqis*, and Cardinal Danielou, in his book *Holy Pagans of the Old Testament*, says that the fact that she belongs both to the gospel and the Qur'an "may be a hidden link that gives reason to hope." The Qur'an portrays her as an idolater, a sun worshipper,[6] though there is nothing in the Hebrew scriptures to tell us that. Danielou instead says that she was actually "already worshipping the true God through the medium of [God's] revelation in the world and in her conscience." In other words, she was already worshipping the true God through the Second Person of the Trinity, Wisdom. Even though she pays tribute to a more perfect revelation in Solomon, she stays "at the level of revelation which was hers." Not only is she a "mystical anticipation of the entry of the Gentiles into the Church," Jesus goes on to say that "she will rise up at the judgment with this generation

---

[4]Jn. 3:8; cf. *Redemptor Hominis,* nn. 6, 11, 12; John Paul II, General Audience, September 9, 1998.

[5]1 Kgs. 10; Mt. 12:42, Lk. 11:31.

[6]Qur'an Sura An-Nami, 27:22–44.

and condemn it" (Mt. 12:42). In other words, she is shown in the future, on the day of Resurrection, sharing the glory of the saints! And Danielou concludes that through this Jesus "testifies to the fact that the pagans who have sought God in sincerity of heart belong to his Church, by what theology calls the baptism of desire, and form part of the elect,"[7] through the Wisdom of the Second Person of the Trinity. One can only imagine what a stir those words might have caused in the Catholic Church in 1956, in the decades before Vatican II, *Nostra Aetate*, and the Declaration on Religious Liberty.

COSMIC REVELATION

One concrete practice to reverence these seeds of the Word that is common in our ashram and Christian ashrams throughout India is the reading of non-Christian sacred texts at the beginning of the liturgy or just before the liturgy begins, a practice that I adopted for my own private prayer. The original proposed Indian rite (which was never fully adopted) after Vatican II had suggested using Indian scriptures *within* the liturgy itself, at the beginning of the Liturgy of the Word and not *before* the liturgy. The explanation of this practice given in the introduction to the *pro manuscripto* version of this proposed Indian rite taught that even if we recognize "only 'seeds of the Word' in these scriptures," the final manifestation of the Word of God in Jesus Christ "did not render these 'seeds' pointless and irrelevant," since Jesus came to fulfill, not to destroy, just as the New Testament did not abolish the Old but helped us to discover richer and deeper meaning in it. The non-Christian scriptures, "even if they represent only a cosmic revelation, still form part of the dynamism of the Word and are better understood when placed in this context."[8]

---

[7] Jean Danielou, *Holy Pagans of the Old Testament* (Baltimore: Helion Press, 1957), 122–125.

[8] *New Orders of the Mass for India* (CBCI Commission for Liturgy, National Catechetical and Liturgical Centre, Bangalore, 1974), 13–14.

Based on that I have an idea for an Easter Vigil service that might embrace some of these elements outside of the Judeo-Christian tradition that perhaps could take place someday, somewhere. We might read the story of creation from the first chapter of Genesis and then read from the Atharva Veda about the *skambha,* the Cosmic Pillar "on whom is firmly founded earth and sky and the air in between," and then sing Psalm 104: "You fixed the earth upon its foundations," for example. Then we could read the story of Abraham sacrificing Isaac, and then something from the epic of Gilgamesh; and then the story of Moses leading the Israelites across the Red Sea followed by the story of Krishna and Arjuna lined up between the Pandavas and the Karuavas before going into battle in the Bhagavad Gita; then sing about the Lord who has "covered himself in glory" in the canticle from the Book of Exodus. And then read from the Book of the Consolation of Israel in the prophet Isaiah, and a passage from the *Tao te Ching*; and then Isaiah 55, and something from the *Dhammapada*; and then the prophet Baruch; and something from *Nityanaimittika-pathavali* of the Jains; and sing Psalm 16: "Lord, you have the words of everlasting life." Then, after we read the beautiful passage from the prophet Ezekiel, perhaps we could conclude by reading something of Socrates' famous culminating speech in Plato's *Symposium*, since it was specifically these Greek thinkers and writers that Justin Martyr was thinking about when he came up with his concept of the "seeds of the Word," just as Paul was thinking of the Greeks when he addressed the Greeks at the Areopagus in Acts 17, telling them that their "unknown God" had raised someone from the dead. And then we could proclaim the story of the Resurrection and tell everyone, like Paul did, that this has all been fulfilled in Jesus!

As Jacques Dupuis explains, and I wholeheartedly agree, we Christians do not and cannot consider other traditions to be equal to Israel in its role in preparing for the Christ event, because other religious traditions do not have an identical meaning in the history of salvation as that of Judaism, or the same relationship with the Christ event. Nevertheless, all these other scriptures were already oriented to that same event and for that reason those others "are all authentic 'evangelical preparations,' even if in an indirect way, and as such are *destined by God*, who directs all of human history to fulfillment in Jesus Christ." This is affirmed in *Lumen Gentium* 16 which states that "whatever good or truth is found amongst them is looked upon by the Church as a preparation for the Gospel. She knows that it is given by Him who enlightens all people so that they may finally have life." Dupuis was even bold enough to say that they "represent *true personal interventions of God* in the history of the nations that point them towards the decisive intervention of God in Jesus Christ."[9]

This echoes *Nostra Aetate*, "The Declaration on the Relation of the Church to Non-Christian Religions" which was proclaimed by Pope Paul VI on October 28, 1965, which states that the Catholic Church "rejects nothing that is true and holy" in other religions. Rather, it regards "those ways of conduct and of life, those precepts and teachings" with sincere reverence. Even though differing in many aspects from the precepts and teachings that the Church holds and sets forth, their teaching, the document admits, "nonetheless often reflect[s] a ray of that Truth which enlightens all people." Then the declaration goes on to exhort Catholics, through "dialogue and collaboration with the followers of other religions," to do three things: *recognize* the good spiritual and moral things found among these people as well as their sociocultural values; *preserve* those good things; and even further than that, actually *promote* them! Recognize, preserve, and promote.

With that in mind, one might also rightly question the use of the word "only" used in the draft of the proposed Indian liturgy, as in "*only* seeds of the Word" and "*only* a cosmic revelation." And what is not mentioned is that not only are those other scriptures "better understood when placed in the context of the Bible," but

---

the Bible too may be better understood when placed in the context of the cosmic revelation and these "seeds of the Word," helping us to see our own tradition as an expression of a larger movement of the Spirit in humanity.

BEAUTY, TRUTH AND GOODNESS

Three points then to sum up our attitude toward recognizing the pro-Christian "seeds of the Word." We followers of Jesus always have the great commission, to "proclaim the good news to the whole creation" (Mk. 16:15). How we do that, of course, is another question, and here the popular apocryphal saying of Saint Francis of Assisi abides: "Preach the good news; use words if necessary." Second, however, it must be said that converting someone to our way of thinking is not the purpose of the dialogue to which we are exhorted. Dialogue, as Panikkar and others in the field of interreligious dialogue would remind us, is more than the sterile crossing of two monologues. True dialogue is the joint search for the shared and the different. True dialogue leads to mutual enrichment from what each partner contributes. True dialogue comes from the desire for mutual understanding of the other's position and the search for a common vocabulary. True dialogue has at its base a recognition that we are not self-sufficient.

Ironically though, and finally, dialogue is actually a very powerful work of evangelization, perhaps the best and most secure face of Christ and the Church.

Bede Griffiths, in an article titled "How I Pray," writing about the Jesus Prayer, explains his understanding of Jesus as Word and expands this theme even further. This Word, this playful Sophia, embraces heaven and earth and is revealed "in different ways and under different names and forms to all humanity." This is the Word, as the prologue of the Gospel of John proclaims, that "enlightens everyone coming into the world," and "though they may not recognize it," Bede says, "it is present to every human being in the depths of their soul. Beyond word and thought, beyond all signs and symbols, this Word is being secretly spoken in every heart in every place and at every time. People may be utterly ignorant of it or may choose to ignore it," but still, Bede says,

> Whenever and wherever anyone responds to truth or love or kindness, to the demand for justice, concern for others, care of those in need, they are responding to the voice of the Word. So also when anyone seeks truth or beauty in science, philosophy, poetry or art, they are responding to the invitation of the Word.[10]

According to Bede, what counts is not so much the name and the form; what counts is the response of the heart to this hidden mystery, a mystery that is present to each one of us in one way or another and awaits our response in faith and hope and love.

We could simply say whenever there is a manifestation of Beauty, Truth, or Goodness, those transcendentals of ancient philosophy, that is already the Word and Wisdom, the Second Person of the Trinity, manifesting. And so this is not just about being in dialogue with other religions: it is about wherever there is beauty, truth, or goodness manifested—be it in a string quartet or a scientific experiment, acts of justice or self-giving love. We see Word and Wisdom manifesting in the self-dedication of a parent, spouse, or friend, the fight for human rights and the betterment of society, and, as the popular saying goes, in "random acts of kindness." We could read the *logos*, even as the Stoics did, in the beauty of the world around us, as Saint Antony, the father of monks, did, saying, "My book, O philosophers, is the book of nature." Or Bernard of Clairvaux, himself a great intellectual, who still poetically proclaimed, "You

---

[10]Bede Griffiths, "How I Pray," from *The One Light: Bede Griffiths' Principal Writings*, ed. Bruno Barnhart (Springfield, IL: Templegate, 2001), 271–272.

will find something more in woods than in books. Woods and
stones will teach you what you can never hear from any master."[11]
This is also why a visit to an art museum can feel like a pilgrimage
and studying good poetry can be *lectio divina*. Wherever there is
beauty, truth, or goodness manifested, there is Word and Wisdom,
the fullness of which we believe was made flesh in Jesus.

This ought to exemplify our attitude and openness even toward so-called atheists and "nones" (those who, for whatever
reason, do not identify with a religious tradition). As Jesus cites
in Matthew and Luke—"Wisdom is vindicated by her deeds" or
"by her children" (Mt. 11:19; Lk. 7:35). We are *exhorted* to be in
dialogue and collaboration with people of good will, not only the
followers of other religions but also noble-hearted scientists and
artists, those who work for justice, and those who care for the
planet. What a great witness it is to our faith and life—and what
authority we ourselves would have!—when and if we recognize,
preserve, and promote spiritual and moral goods and sociocultural
values wherever we find them, not only claiming them for Christ,
but claiming them *as* Christ, as christic, as a manifestation of the
Word and Wisdom, the fullness of which we believe was made
flesh in Lord Jesus.

This is nothing new. St. Albert the Great and his most famous
student St. Thomas Aquinas, who is considered to be the greatest
theologian of Catholicism and the author of our own perennial
philosophy, beautifully exemplified truly catholic (i.e., universal)
minds in the sense that they were open to every good influence
and any right idea. They taught at a time when many Catholic
theologians were reacting against influences coming from Asia or
so-called "pagan" writers. And yet they drew on such suspicious
sources as Pseudo-Dionysius and the Greek apophatic theology;
Albert particularly defended theses on the incomprehensibility of

[11]Ep. 107, *The Letters of St. Bernard of Clairvaux*, trans. Bruno Scott James (Chicago: Henry Regnery, 1953), 156.

God. Besides drawing on Plato and Cicero, they also introduced the writings of Aristotle, which they got from Jewish thinkers such as the Rabbi Moses Maimonides and the Andalusian poet and philosopher Avicebron,[12] and Muslim scholars such as Averroes and Avicenna—in other words, the writings of another pagan philosopher as mediated by scholars who were considered infidels. Even when they disagreed with a thinker, they did so respectfully, with reasoned discourse. As Bishop Barron often points out, "At a time when adherents of different religions often gaze at each other suspiciously, the Thomas who happily dialogued with pagan philosophers, Jewish rabbis, Muslim sages, and Christian heretics calls us back to an attitude of broad-minded respect."[13]

In 1958 the German Thomist theologian Josef Pieper presciently wrote about the openness that marked the attitude of Thomas Aquinas and Albert the Great, saying that we needed to have that same openness because there are new territories that needed to be explored. He names three: first of all, there are the new realms opened up by physics and biology; then there is "the dimension of the psyche brought into view by the findings of depth psychology"; finally, Pieper points to the wisdom of the East, "ready for and apparently in want of absorption into the intellectual structure of Christian philosophical interpretation and the Christian way of life—or it may be that it is we who need enrichment through this wisdom, in a quite particular manner."[14]

Let me reiterate, in keeping again with how we might learn aspects of the universality of the Trinity from other traditions that have until now remained inchoate in our own: it may be that it is we who need enrichment through this wisdom outside the visible boundaries of the Church.

---

[12]As the eleventh-century Jewish philosopher Solomon ibn Gabirol was known. He is credited with having coined the name "Kabbalah."

[13]Robert Barron, *Vibrant Paradoxes: The Both/And of Catholicism* (Skokie, IL: Word on Fire Catholic Ministries, 2016), 48.

[14]Joseph Pieper, *The Silence of St. Thomas* (New York: Pantheon, 1957), 104.

ATHANASIUS: THE WORD
AND THE TAO

St. Athanasius was a fourth-century theologian and one of the four doctors of the Eastern and Western Church along with Ambrose, John Chrysostom, and Augustine. He was the bishop of Alexandria, and an intimate of Saint Antony of the Desert. Antony was a great champion of Athanasius's teaching, and when he died, Athanasius inherited one of the two sheepskins that Antony left as his only legacy. Athanasius returned the favor by writing the *Life of Antony*, which was widely read and very influential in shaping Christian anthropology as well as promoting the Christian monastic life. He is also credited with being the first to name the same twenty-seven books of the New Testament that we have today.

Above all, Athanasius is considered the great theologian of the incarnation of the *Logos*. When he was a young cleric, he took part in the Council of Nicaea, the council that gave us the definitive definition of Jesus being *homoousios*—one substance (or, as we say now, "consubstantial") with the Father. This was mainly addressed against the Arian heresy, which was prevalent at the time, and against which Athanasius continued to fight for most of his ecclesial career, even suffering exile and persecution for it. The Arian heresy taught that the *Logos*—the Word, the Second Person of the Trinity—was not true God but was instead a "created god," a creature halfway between a God and a human being.

Remember that Philo and his Greek antecedents always felt it was necessary to maintain the distinction between the perfect idea and imperfect matter, between God and creation. And that's why the *logos* was necessary, Philo taught: because God cannot come into contact with matter. Christianity turned philosophy on its ear by claiming that God has come into contact with matter. Worse yet, Christians claim that God has *become* matter! "The Word was made flesh and dwelt among us" (Jn. 1:14). John, Athanasius, and orthodox Christianity were claiming, for the first time in history, that this *logos*—the Creator and sustainer, the pattern and ordering principle of nature—"was made flesh and dwelt among us," that the "fullness of the godhead dwelt in Jesus bodily" (Col. 2:9), that Jesus was the perfect embodiment of the divine universal knowledge.

When John spoke of the *Logos*, it was no longer in riddles, as if we could glimpse only little traces and hints in nature. This very *Logos* that Heraclitus said would always prove to be un-comprehending, the very *Tao* that Lao Tzu had said no one in the world would be able to understand, was accessible, tangible, and made human. John wrote that he had *seen him*; he had beheld his glory and heard the words he spoke, and laid his head on his breast. That's why we read the prologue of John at Christmas, and what we are gazing at in the manger, this little boy-child, is the embodiment and summation of the plan for the universe. As one book title goes, *Christ the Eternal Tao*—Christ *is* this eternal *Tao*. So we hear in Paul's Colossians canticle, "In him all things in heaven and earth were created . . . all things have been created through him and for him," in this light, because the Christ is Word and Wisdom made flesh. Paul also says that in him "the fullness of God was pleased to dwell" (Col. 1:15, 19). We could equally say that the fullness of Word and Wisdom, the fullness of the intelligence principle of the universe, dwelt bodily in Jesus.

Yet this intelligent principle, this *Logos* or *Tao*, is not a big flashy thing. It's not a monstrosity of a structure or a great superimposing force. Like the *Tao*, so the Word, the *Logos*, is like water: "nurturing the ten thousand things without competing, flowing into places people scorn," like the newborn babe at Christmas, as soft as water. That's what Athanasius was fighting for against the Arians.

The contemporary philosopher Ken Wilber writes about the difference between *ascending* and *descending* religions, traditions that are climbing the ladder away from earth to heaven and traditions that are very much earthbound. Wilber suggests that harmony is found in the union of the ascending and the descending currents, and not in a kind of brutal war between the two. And he says that only when ascending and descending are united can both be saved. "And those who do not contribute to this union not only destroy the only Earth we have, but forfeit the only heaven they might otherwise embrace."[15]

I think many might find Christianity to be one of those *ascending* religions, because most people would say that the *telos*, the ultimate goal, of Christianity is for the body to die and the soul to go to heaven. But from my understanding, Wilber actually just stumbled onto Christianity, because this is specifically what happens in Christianity, or at least what is supposed to happen: it is a union of the ascending and descending. While we are busy ascending to God, God is revealed in descending, in the incarnation of Word and Wisdom.

The renowned Anglican bishop and scripture scholar N. T. Wright says the rather shocking thing that "the traditional preaching about everyone having a 'soul' which needs saving" is "almost hopelessly misleading." Ultimate salvation according to the Christian scriptural tradition, he states, rather controversially, "is not in heaven"! Ultimate salvation is "in the resurrection into the combined reality of a new heaven and a new earth." The end, the *telos*, according to Christian scriptures, is a new heaven and a new earth; the end is eschatological integration—not just eschaton but eschatological integration.[16] This is what we learn from the incarnation of the Word. So maybe we are not just an ascending religion after all.

Why that matters and how this ties into Athanasius is first of all because it is from Athanasius that we get the famous dictum that we hear in the Office of Readings each Christmastide, from his writing *De Incarnatione*—"On the Incarnation of the Word": "The

---

[15]Ken Wilber, *A Brief History of Everything* (Boston: Shambhala, 1996), 12–13.

[16]Rt. Rev. Prof. N. T. Wright, "Mind, Spirit, Soul and Body: All for One and One for All: Reflections on Paul's Anthropology in His Complex Contexts," for the Society of Christian Philosophers: Regional Meeting, Fordham University, March 18, 2011, 2.

Word of God became a human being so that we might be made God." The "fundamental idea of Athanasius's entire theological battle was precisely that God is accessible," and that through our communion with Jesus "we can truly be united to God."[17] God really is *Emmanu-el*—God-with-us.

It also matters because it is out of this that we get the notion of *kata physin*—"according to nature." When Athanasius writes *The Life of Antony,* the words used to describe Antony coming out of the tombs (#14) are very important. After his years of asceticism, Antony is healthy and psychically sound. The words in Greek Athanasius uses are *kata physin*—Antony is "according to nature," meaning that Antony's life of asceticism and virtue has led him to physical vigor as well as psychological balance. Athanasius is showing through Antony what a deified human being is like, and he is still *kata physin*—"according to nature." Our humanity is not destroyed; we are brought to our human perfection by grace.

In other words, in the deified saint the Word is made flesh again.

As Pope Benedict iterated in *Deus Caritas Es*: "Those who draw near to God do not withdraw from other people, but rather they become truly close to them."[18] As Augustine wrote, "Love calls us to things of this world." The Word was made flesh and continually becomes flesh—in us. We are to share the divinity of Christ who came to share in our humanity—through the Word and Wisdom of God.

So the Silence speaks many words, but the Father speaks only one Word, one Word that sums up all those other words—Jesus, in whom "the fullness of the godhead dwelt bodily" and who we say was the Word and Wisdom made flesh, all those other partial words brought to their completion in this human form. This is Jesus not only as a deity, but as fully human too, as the Cosmic

---

[17]Pope Benedict XVI, *Great Christian Thinkers: From the Early Church through the Middle Ages* (Minneapolis: Fortress Press, 2011), 41.

[18]Pope Benedict, *Deus Caritas Es*, n. 42.

Person who holds all things together in himself, the archetype and the goal, the blueprint behind being human.

There's a beautiful phrase of Saint Clare of Assisi that says Jesus "is the radiance of eternal glory" and "the brightness of eternal light and the mirror without blemish." And so she advises, "Gaze upon that mirror each day . . . and continually study your face in it."[19]

[19]Clare of Assisi, from the fourth letter to Agnes of Prague, in *The Lady: Clare of Assisi, Early Documents*, ed. and trans. Regis J. Armstrong, OFM Cap. (Hyde Park, NY: New City Press, 2006), 55.

8

Sacrament of History

A further step in our rediscovery of the Second Person of the Trinity, and the corresponding energy that goes with it, is a new sense of time and history and an appreciation of time's forward movement. If there is an intelligence behind the universe—called *Logos*-Word, *Sophia*-Wisdom, the *Tao*—this implies an intentionality and a direction, a plan. Saint Paul will call it an economy, an *oikonomian*, perhaps what Tao te Ching calls "the way of heaven and earth." This implies even an ultimate goal, a telos, a whole reason for being.

Here let's point out a difference between the prophetic traditions and the mystical traditions. Judaism, Christianity, and Islam would be considered prophetic traditions in the sense that they are based on a revealed message, an intervention by the Divine into history. The Asian traditions of Hinduism, Buddhism, and Taoism are sometimes referred to as the mystical traditions because they are much more focused on interiority and psychological transformation than on outward phenomena. I want to rush in to say that there is a little of each in the other, as in the yin-yang symbol of Taoism in which there is a dot of dark in the light half and a dot of light in the dark. Meaning that there is obviously a mystical tradition in Christianity, Judaism, or Islam. Likewise, there is some sense of history and care for creation in Hinduism, Buddhism, and Taoism. What we are always looking for is a sharing in the riches of both the so-called East and West, the prophetic and the mystical, for a fuller picture, what Bede Griffiths called the "marriage of east and west."

In this moment, we are speaking about a sense of the *dynamism* of history in the prophetic traditions. As Bede Griffiths describes it, "In the oriental tradition, time is always conceived to be cyclical. Everything moves in cycles." But in the Christian vision, and I want to say that the same applies equally to the Jew and Muslim, "time is not cyclical but linear. The universe has a beginning in time and moves through time to an end, an 'eschaton.'"[1]

RECAPITULATION

Because of this emphasis on the linear, the forward progress of history, we come to see Jesus and "the Christ event" as a high point on this line, even as *the* high point in evolution, the evolution of human consciousness and the spiritual evolution of the human race. Bruno refers to Jesus as a "noonday"; the Christ event is a decisive moment in the forward trajectory of evolution, a high point with which we are still trying to catch up.

We already see evidence of this way of thinking in Saint Paul's writings. In the Letters to the Romans and the Colossians Paul writes about "the mystery hidden before all ages" (Col. 1:26), and in the Letter to the Galatians he writes that "when the fullness of time had come, God sent his Son born of a woman" (Gal. 4:4). Put those two images together and we see that there's been a movement in history that has led up to this: the mystery hidden from all ages (the full revelation of the Wisdom of the divine plan) now, in the fullness of time (this moment of the Christ event), has been

---

[1]Bede Griffiths, 1989 Hibbert Lecture on the BBC, quoted in *The One Light: Bede Griffiths' Principal Writings*, ed. Bruno Barnhart (Springfield, IL: Templegate, 2001), 358–359.

revealed in the Word being made flesh. The mystery hidden from all ages is revealed in this child born of a woman who is the perfect incarnation of the divine plan.

Then, in his Letter to the Ephesians, Paul speaks of the end of this trajectory. In the person of Jesus, God has made "known to us the mystery of his will, according to his purpose, which he set forth in Christ as a plan"—an *oikonomian*, an economy—"for the fullness of time." And what is that plan, that economy? "To unite all things in him, things in heaven and things on earth" (Eph. 1:9b–10).

Besides *oikonomian*, the operative word in that verse from Ephesians is the Greek word *anakephalaios*. This gets translated in various ways: "gather up all things," "unite all things." The Greek root is literally *kepha,* "head." Paul coined this phrase to express the meaning of the Incarnation; as the Jerusalem Bible translates it, more literally, it was God's plan to "bring everything together under Christ as Head." In Italian, the word *anakephalaios* is translated by a helpful term, one that passes into theology: *ricapitulare*—"recapitulate." (The Italian *capo* means "head" or "leader.") Recapitulation is a theme that is mentioned briefly in the writings of Justin Martyr, but was especially a major theme of the second-century theologian Irenaeus of Lyons. "Recapitulate" is first of all a rhetorical term meaning to summarize or sum up an argument by going over the principal points, to bring a capstone to an argument. It's also a biological term that refers to development and growth—and let's embrace that organic meaning as well.

In Christology, recapitulate takes on another meaning. Alongside the idea that Christ came to save us and redeem us, a theology also developed that focuses on recapitulation: the incarnation as the highpoint of this linear movement, the summation of an entire trajectory, the incarnational trajectory. The Second Person of the Trinity wasn't made flesh simply to fix a mistake; Jesus is also, mainly, the high point of an evolutionary line. The mystery of recapitulation for Irenaeus is not simply the repairing of a plan that had gone wrong in the Fall. From the beginning of time, all humankind was, and indeed all creation was, preordained and predestined to reach its highpoint in the incarnation of the *Logos*, with or without the Fall. Creation was always intended for this, that the Sophia of God would be made flesh. What's more, when the Second Person of the Trinity incarnates in the substance of creation, not just the human person but all of creation is re-created and renewed. This makes Christ not only the head of the Church but the highpoint of material creation and the keystone of the universe. Christ as the "heavenly man" not only leads humanity back home but, with humankind, all the cosmos as well.

Without denying that God speaks in "many and various ways" (Heb. 1:1) in the course of history, Christians also believe there was and is something unique in the course of history about this Christ event, the fullness of the godhead dwelling bodily in this person of Jesus. Obviously, this is not something that Hindus and Buddhists (let alone Jews and Muslims) believe—that Jesus was/is the highpoint of evolution and the capstone of the universe—but at least this gives us another way to explain who we believe Jesus is and what we believe happened in the Christ event.

At the same time, the notion that a human being could be the perfect embodiment of ultimate Wisdom is not unheard of in other religious traditions. In the Kabbalah tradition of Judaism there is the idea of *adam kadmon* (sometimes called *adam elyon*), the primordial man after whom Adam was fashioned. The sixteenth-century kabbalist Isaac Luria described *adam kadmon* as the most perfect manifestation of God that the human mind can contemplate. It is usually imaged anthropomorphically, giving a divine symbolism to the human body. Some will associate him with the coming messiah; still others, the disciples of the seventeenth-century Turkish messianic leader Shabbetai Zevi, thought that Zevi himself was the *adam kadmon*.

In Islam, the great twelfth-century Sufi mystic philosopher Ibn 'Arabi taught the concept of *al-Insan al-Kamil*, the perfect man by whom God is revealed to God's own self. Ibn 'Arabi associated this with the Prophet Muhammed who he taught was the archetype of the universe and humanity.

It may be a further stretch, but in Mahāyāna Buddhism also there is the teaching about the *trikāya*, the three bodies of the Buddha. The first of the bodies is called the *Nirmānakāya*, the Buddha in human form. And the Buddha himself is said to have taught that "those who have seen the Buddha have seen the dharma"— "dharma" here meaning not only the Buddha's own teachings but also the order and law of the cosmos (could this be an equivalent of *logos*?)—and "those who have seen the dharma have seen the Buddha" since the Buddha is a manifestation of the truth that is dharma. So it is not unprecedented that a religious tradition would come to see the divine plan for the cosmos fulfilled and perfected—dare we say recapitulated?—at a particular moment, in a particular human being, and in the human person in general.

ADAM AND JESUS

Irenaeus draws out a long comparison between Adam and Jesus, working out a parallelism between the two in minute detail to show how Jesus "recapitulates" Adam, brings to completion the plan begun in the primal human. He is commenting on this passage from 1 Corinthians: "Thus it is written, 'The first man, Adam, became a living being'; the last Adam became a life-giving spirit. But it is not the spiritual that is first, but the physical, and then the spiritual. The first man was from the earth, a man of dust; the second man is from heaven" (1 Cor. 15:45–47). So, Irenaeus says, just as Adam was fashioned from earth, so was Jesus formed from the very same earth. Like Adam, Jesus had no human father. Most important, Jesus re-does and redeems Adam's temptation and disobedience by being victorious in obedience. This is not just Adam's renewal; it's also a restoration of the human race to the glory that had been intended for it from the beginning—and there's our recapitulation. Christ assumes Adam's headship by gathering all of Adam's progeny into himself. This, Irenaeus says, is why the genealogy of Jesus in the third chapter of the Gospel of Luke begins with Joseph, the husband of Mary, and works backwards to Adam, to show that Jesus recapitulates Adam himself and all his descendants.[2]

Remember we are also still speaking here about the Second Person of the Trinity—the Word and Wisdom—even before the birth of Jesus. Now in Irenaeus this Second Person takes on some of the qualities of creator as well, as we saw happened also in the writings about Sophia. The Word is the creator of the world who governs and disposes all things and then is "crucified in the whole universe and imprinted in the form of a cross." The presence of Word and Wisdom stretches throughout all creation, holding every part in existence. Remember Paul's Canticle from Colossians: "He holds all creation together in himself." Here note also the cross as a universal symbol, the cross of Holy Wisdom imprinted on the whole cosmos.

> It was necessary and proper that, once made visible,
> [Christ] should make manifest the universality of his cross,
> so as to show plainly, in visible form, this work of his,
> that it is he who makes the height to shine—that is, what
>   is in heaven;
> and contains the depth—that is, what is under earth;
> and, by stretching out, extends the length from East to
>   West,
> and guides the Northern wastes and the Southern vastness,
> and calls all those everywhere dispersed to the knowledge
>   of the Father.[3]

SPIRIT AND HISTORY

Bruno Barnhart picks up on this theme in soaring poetic sentences at the beginning of his book *The Future of Wisdom* where he

---

[2]Cf. Irenaeus, *Against Heresies*, III.18.1; III.22.3. See Denis Minns, OP, *Irenaeus* (Washington, DC: Georgetown University Press, 1994), 92–94.

[3]Irenaeus, "Demonstration of the Apostolic Teaching," #34, quoted in Minns, 93.

writes that the two great principles he will be presenting are spirit and history. "Spirit" here is not referring just to the Holy Spirit. Bruno is espousing the tripartite anthropology that understands "spirit" as an anthropological element, a part of human being, which we will explore more below. "Spirit" here refers to that third element of the human person, beyond body and soul, "the interior or spiritual or divine aspect of humanity."

Spirit also stands for transcendence, mysticism and the mystical, eternity rather than time, the ancient and the Asian—Hinduism, Buddhism, Taoism. In contrast, there is history and historicity, which encompass prophecy, incarnation, time as a sacrament, the West and modernity—Judaism, Christianity, and Islam. These two—spirit and history—become the vertical and horizontal axes of the cross: transcendence as the upright and historicity as the crossbeam.[4] In imaging it thus, instead of seeing these two as antagonistic—the mystical and the prophetic, transcendence and historicity, Asia and Israel—Bruno sees them as complementary, as two dimensions ultimately meeting "in Jesus Christ, in whom divine Spirit enters newly and decisively into the human person and in human history, the decisive meeting point of God and creation, at which is initiated *a new human history, impregnated with the unitive Divine reality.*"[5]

The Christ event is a decisive meeting point at which a new human history is inaugurated. Spirit and history, the mystical and the prophetic are not antagonistic; they are complementary. If they meet in Jesus and the Christ event, this means that they also intersect as horizontal and vertical dimensions within each human person—in *us*. As both of these axes are operative in the story of Jesus and are aspects of the Christ event, so they are operative in each of us who are made in the image of God.

So we meet the energy of the Second Person of the Trinity in

---

[4]Bruno credits this to Karl Rahner.
[5]Bruno Barnhart, *The Future of Wisdom* (New York: Continuum, 2007), 20. Emphasis mine.

ourselves: we too hold this intersection of transcendence and historicity, of mysticism and prophecy, of East and West, of interiority and involvement, within us, because they are aspects of being human in the image of God.

EVOLUTION AND DEVELOPMENT

If we were to grasp the idea of time as a sacrament of history, and the birth of Jesus as a decisive high point on this line, this then "consecrates" evolution. As Ilia Delio writes, we can "locate Christ at the heart of the whole evolutionary process: from cosmic evolution to biological evolution to evolution of human consciousness and culture."[6]

Irenaeus mentions several times the idea of development. I suggest that this is his version of evolution, the gradual development of the human person who was not created perfect but grew, from Adam to Jesus, in perfection. That's why the continuity from Adam to Jesus is so important, because that perfection happens in Jesus. Referring to the myth of the Fall in the Garden of Eden, Irenaeus says that Satan struck the first blow when the earth creature was still weak and immature, before he had time to grow strong enough to bear the likeness of God.[7] And if Adam had a sin, it was precisely impatience with the timing of the divine *oikonomian*. Adam snatched at immortality and likeness to God before he was able to bear them. He snatched at immortality and likeness to God before God was ready to bestow them.[8] According to Paul, in the great *kenosis* hymn in the Letter to the Philippians, of course, this is exactly what Christ Jesus did *not* do: "Christ Jesus did not deem equality with God something to be grasped at but emptied himself" (Phil. 2:6). And Irenaeus says that every sin (in us) is exactly that:

---

[6]Ilia Delio, *Christ in Evolution* (Maryknoll, NY: Orbis Books, 2008), 174.
[7]Cf. Irenaeus, "Demonstration of the Apostolic Teaching," 12, 16.
[8]Minns, *Irenaeus*, 98.

trying to achieve something outside of the divine plan or outside of the timeframe set by God.[9] So even though Satan intervened and struck the first blow when the earth creature was still weak and immature, God does not change the plan or hurry the plan, that the gulf would be bridged between the uncreated God and the created order in the perfecting of the "earth creature." After the Fall, humankind was left in bondage until its development, until its evolution, had been completed.[10]

What it means that Christ Jesus is the "new Adam" is that Jesus is that fully developed human being, the fully developed "earth creature," the noonday of human development. Jesus the Christ, the Word-Made-Flesh, is fully the image and likeness of God because in his humanity, in his flesh, he was totally responsive and open to and receptive of the transforming Spirit. When Jesus confronts Satan in his temptation in the desert, *not* succumbing to the temptation to be impatient with God's plan, he does so as the same earth creature whom Satan defeated at the beginning of the story. Hence, he is the new Adam, fully mature and developed, fully in the image and likeness of God. And this time Satan does not win.

So here we have more than hints at a forward movement of history, history become salvation history in the Christian way of thinking, in Irenaeus's idea of recapitulation: "When the fullness of time had come, God sent his Son born of a woman" (Gal. 4:4). When the fullness of time came, at the right time according to God's plan, the Second Person of the Trinity, the Word and Wisdom of God, became flesh—which is what was intended all along! That was the *telos*. Or maybe it's better to say that was only the *scopos*, the proximate goal. The ultimate *telos* is a new heaven and a new earth. As Paul says, the end is "that God may be all in all" (1 Cor. 15:28).

One last recapitulation of Irenaeus: although there is a great gulf between the uncreated God and the created order, the whole

---

[9]Cf. *Against Heresies,* IV.38, 4.
[10]Cf. *Against Heresies,* III.23.1, 6.

wonder of the economy of the divine plan is that from the beginning God meant for the gulf between spirit and matter, the divine and the created, to be bridged by perfecting the human being, Adam, in his own image and likeness, and in lifting that creature up to friendship and communion with himself through a new Adam—Jesus, Word and Wisdom made flesh. This is the center of what gets celebrated over and over during Christmastide, that at a certain moment in history, this happened, as the proclamation of the prologue of the Gospel of John tells us, "The Word was made flesh and dwelt among us." And so we pray that we may be "found in the likeness of him in whom our nature is united to you."[11]

Because we believe that because there is intelligence behind creation, God's perfect plan, we also don't think that time is chaos, or going round and round in circles, nor that evolution is random, but that it is all going somewhere, and going somewhere good—going to the Reign of God, when God will be all in all. That's its *telos*. This is especially helpful in our dialogue with Judaism and Islam, because it is a certain gift of the prophetic traditions in general to believe that time is not an illusion, not something to be escaped. Our complement to transcendence and otherworldly mysticism is the assertion that time is a sacrament, history is going somewhere, and where it's going is the Reign of God.

EVOLUTIONARY OPTIMISM VERSUS ESCHATOLOGICAL HOPE

Another place in Saint Paul where the question of time and its telos is operative is in the fifteenth chapter of the Letter to the Corinthians—and it is of no little consequence that this is in the section about the resurrection of the dead. We quoted the last phrase of this verse, a few paragraphs above. Here Paul says, "When all things are subjected to him, then the Son himself will also be subjected

---

[11]Collect for the Saturday after Epiphany.

to him who put all things in subjection under him, that God may be all in all" (1 Cor. 15:28). This is sometimes translated that God may be "everything in everything." N. T. Wright says, "This is one of the clearest statements of the very center of the future-oriented New Testament worldview." But he also points out how important it is that we keep the accent on the "will," in other words, on the future tense, not God *is* all in all. That is the problem with what Wright calls "evolutionary optimism" and pantheism: God is not all in all, not yet. "Until the final victory over evil, and particularly over death, this moment has not yet arrived. To suggest that it has is to collude with evil and with death itself."[12]

The problem with evolutionary optimism[13] is that it doesn't take into account that it is not always a straight line. As C. S. Lewis makes clear in *The Great Divorce,* every road forks in two and two again, and we always have to choose. And sometimes we do not choose well, because there is evil and there is sin. So every now and then we have to backtrack and pick up the right trail again. Christianity's problem with pantheism is that it wants to say everything is God, or that God is everything; and this just does not abide with orthodox Christian thinking, nor with scripture.

So what is the relationship of God to creation? For orthodox Christianity, it matters that creation is other than God, that creation is not God. We do not agree with the dualists, such as the Gnostics and the Manicheans that Irenaeus and Augustine were warring with respectively, who suggest that if God made something that is not God's own self, then it must be less than good, or even evil. At the same time, we do not express it as our nondual friends do: if in the beginning God is all there is, how can there be room for anything or anyone else? At some point, yes, God *will* be all in all, but that moment is not yet.

---

[12]N. T. Wright, *Surprised by Hope: Rethinking Heaven, the Resurrection, and the Mission of the Church* (New York: HarperCollins, 2008), 101–102.

[13]Wright calls it "Teilhardian evolutionary optimism," which I take exception with though he is obviously more intelligent than I, but let's take the Teilhardian adjective out for the moment.

Another solution that was offered by the great German theologian Jürgen Moltmann was a recovery of the fascinating notion that comes from the Jewish rabbinic tradition, *zimzum* (or *tsimtsum*), a Hebrew word that means "contraction." This is another teaching of the kabbalist Isaac Luria, that in order for creation to take place, God had to in some sense make space for it by withdrawing, contracting: "God withdraws from a certain dimension of reality in order to allow the non-God to exist."[14]

None of those explanations work from our scriptures. Creation is a work of love, as Wright says, and love always involves something other than itself, hence something other than God. That same love then "allows creation to be itself, sustaining it in providence and wisdom, but not overpowering it." So instead of contracting, Wright suggests that "God creates new space for there to be things that are genuinely other than God." Hence: the world is good—but incomplete, and God intends in the end to fill all creation with the divine presence and love. Here is our new heavens and new earth, mentioned three times in scripture, in the prophet Isaiah, in the First Letter of Peter, and at the very end of the Bible in the Book of Revelation.[15]

> One day, when all the forces of rebellion have been defeated and the creation responds freely and gladly to the love of its creator, God will fill it with himself so that it will *both* remain an independent being, other than God, *and also* be flooded with God's own life.[16]

In other words, *God will be all in all.* That's our eschatological hope.

Remember Panikkar's idea of "person." Person always implies relationship, and as there is a *perichoresis* among the persons of the Trinity—mutually giving way to each other—so there is a

[14]Arthur Green, *Ehyeh: A Kabbalah for Tomorrow* (Woodstock, VT: Jewish Lights, 2003), 25.
[15]Is. 65:17; 2 Pt. 3:13; Rev. 21:1.
[16]Wright, *Surprised by Hope*, 101–102.

cosmo-the-andric perichoresis: God, humanity, and the cosmos always in relationship.[17]

Remember, too, my suggestion of God being more like the Great Mother in the sense that, like a mother, God gives birth to the child (creation) and the child grows in autonomy and independence, but also in the sense that in order for us to recover what we lost in terms of dynamism—spiritual, psychological, and even physical—we have to return to the Mother.

The women mystics understand this. Here is Hildegard of Bingen from the *Scivias*:

> Through the fountain-fullness of the Word came the embrace of God's maternal love, which has nourished us into life and is our help in perils, and is a deepest and sweetest charity and prepares us for penitence.[18]

ALL SHALL BE WELL

I want to end this meditation on time and history with the example of another woman mystic, Julian of Norwich. Julian lived during a period of great suffering and uncertainty. The Hundred Years' War between England and France began before she was born and continued long after she died. Famine was prevalent throughout England as often happens during wartime. Perhaps most catastrophic of all, she wrote during a time of pandemic: the decimation of much of Europe's population by the bubonic plague. Three outbreaks occurred in her own city during her lifetime. All in all, the pain must have seemed overwhelming: suffering was everywhere and many attributed the horror to the wrath of God.

So it is all the more noteworthy that her spiritual theological

---

[17]Raimundo Panikkar, *Il silenzio del Buddha: Un ateismo religioso* (Milan: Mondadori, 2006), 170–171. My translation.

[18]Hildegard of Bingen, *Scivias* II, 2,4., trans. Mother Columba Hart and Jane Bishop (New York: Paulist Press, 1990), 162.

response isn't one of despair or judgment, but of love, solidarity, and hope.

Julian appealed to God for three things: a stronger understanding of Christ's passion; the experiences that a body and soul experience in death (including attack by devils and administration of the last rites) but without actually expiring, so that she might learn to live more mindful of God; and for three "wounds": absolute contrition, kind compassion, and steadfast longing toward God.

As if to answer her prayer, Julian herself nearly died, from the plague or some other illness. Everyone around her despaired of her life, and she too believed she was dying. The last rites were administered to her. Then a wonderful thing happened. Julian had what we might call a near-death experience, and one day at the height of her illness, between four and nine in the afternoon and evening, she received fifteen "showings" or revelations. She says that heaven opened to her; she beheld Christ in his glory; and she saw the meaning and power of his sufferings. In her thirteenth showing, Julian received a comforting answer to a question that had troubled her for a long time:

> In my folly before this time I often wondered why, through the great prescient wisdom of God, the beginning of sin was not prevented. For then it seemed to me that all would have been well.
>
> This impulse to think this was greatly to be shunned; nevertheless I mourned and sorrowed on this account, unreasonably, lacking discretion. But Jesus, who in this vision informed me about everything needful to me, answered with these words and said: Sin is necessary, but all will be well, and all will be well, and every kind of thing will be well.[19]

---

[19] *Julian of Norwich, Showings,* trans. *Edmund Colledge, OSA, and James Walsh, SJ* (New York: Paulist Press, 1978), Thirteenth Revelation, twenty-seventh chapter, 224–225. The original Middle English of this sentence is actually, "Sin is behovely, but all shall be well and all shall be well and all manner of thing shall be well."

With all that had gone on in her life and around her, her belief that "all shall be well" was not the hysterical optimism of someone putting on rose-colored glasses or sticking their head in the sand pretending all this bad stuff will go away, but the voice of one who has deeply experienced suffering and tried to make sense of it. And the way she does so is through a brutally honest trust in the love of God.

In a seemingly paradoxical move, Julian, an anchoress who lived in isolation, tells us about a God who is essentially relational: the Father, Son, and Holy Spirit in relationship with one another and in relationship with humanity through Jesus. She uses familial language to describe God and Jesus and their relationship to humanity: mother, father, brother, and spouse. God, in this sense, is immanent and intimate, and has created a world in which everything that exists, exists through the love of God. God makes, loves, and protects, and thus the relational love and action of God permeate all of life.

This dynamism of history is already our bridge to the Third Person. However, as we end our discussion of the Second Person, I remind you of the challenge I posed earlier. Our Muslim sisters and brothers refer to Jews and Christians as being, like them, *ahl al-Kitab*, the People of the Book. But if we are to be not simply People of the Book but truly *People of the Word*, People of the Second Person of the Trinity, we will need to realize the full extent of what that term encompasses, and be children of *Sophia-Logos-Tao*, recognizing the *semina verbi*, seeds of the Word, and traces of Wisdom in the sacrament of time and history.

Before we move into our rediscovery of the Third Person, let's meditate on how we have articulated our rediscovery of the Second Person, and of how we are in a real way formed according to God's image. The Wisdom of God—the *Tao*, the *Logos*—is the very pattern and archetype of creation, the intentionality and even the directionality of the cosmos. In the deepest infrastructure of my being too, perhaps even embedded in my genetic coding, is the divine plan, the way of heaven and earth. This is why we make the inward journey of contemplative prayer and meditation, to discover this law written on our hearts which, perhaps with an awareness that is not (yet?) understanding, will give us a direction and intention too.

What is the divine intention and directionality written on my heart? Can I trust in what Teilhard calls "the slow work of God"?

9

Thought Becomes Fire

Just as there is a danger in the First Person and its energy—returning to the warm womb of the Great Mother and remaining there—there also is a danger in the Second Movement if Word and Wisdom don't have dynamism. This is why the idea of development and the forward movement of the history of Word and Wisdom are so important. As Teilhard taught us, "We're going somewhere." The Christian *logos* can easily become encased, as Bruno Barnhart thought it did, "within a container of Greek philosophical thought." And if there are problems with Greek philosophical thought, one is that it tends toward a dualism between spirit and matter, and a second is in the way it subordinates and even excludes *psyche* and the feminine dimension of the human person.

There are those who argue that it was providential for Judaism to meet Greek thought in the Alexandrians in the last centuries before the Common Era, giving the Hebrew mythological language a philosophical and rational language. And there are others who think it was also providential that Christianity first went to what we now know as Europe via Greece instead of going farther into Asia, as recorded in the Acts of the Apostles—"they were prevented from going into Asia" (see Acts 6:16). Bruno, on the other hand, thought that the "crystalline Greek theology" actually "arrested the historical and affective *dynamism* that is intrinsic to Christianity."[1] (He is also not the only one to lament that this happened again later on in the Middle Ages when Scholasticism eclipsed the sapiential, wisdom tradition of monasticism.) Overall, perhaps the same could be said for masculine rationality in general—it has a tendency to encase and arrest.

So we have to be cautious about the *Logos* (and perhaps even Sophia!) getting encased in thought. We are now all about recovering the affective dynamism that is intrinsic to Christianity.

There is salvation: Just as "there is a central well within us where thoughts disappear into the unitive depths"—the Eastern, contemplative movement, the return to the Mother, Plotinus and Neo-Platonism's flight of the alone to the Alone, the *Word into Silence*—so there is a movement outward, "an ardent boundary within us *where thought becomes fire.*"[2] And this is the Third Movement, which Bruno called the Music and which he saw in this present age, the age of the Spirit, when Word and Wisdom, *Logos* and *Sophia* and the Tao, become energy. Bruno was one of those people who was still almost giddy about Karl Rahner and the Second Vatican Council. Pope John's vision and the council that grew from it ushered in the era when Catholicism truly became a world church and no longer a European export. As Rahner wrote, though Jesus is always the heart of the message, in becoming a world church it proclaims a message to the world in a new way, more unconditionally and more courageously. And in both the messenger and the message, "something new has happened, something irreversible, something that remains."[3]

What this has to do with the Third Person of the Trinity is that Rahner is proclaiming a third age which "with its new pluralism

---

[1] Bruno Barnhart, *Second Simplicity: The Inner Shape of Christianity* (New York: Paulist Press, 1999), 56.

[2] Ibid., 90. This also is the danger of the East's movement back to the One, to the Silence.

[3] Karl Rahner, "The Abiding Significance of the Second Vatican Council," in *Theological Investigations* 20, trans. E Quinn (Spring Valley, NY: Crossroad, 1986), 90–109.

and confident openness might be called the age of the Spirit. We can feel here a wave of optimism at the time of the council."[4] In the greater picture, along with the likes of others such as the late Catholic theologian Ewert Cousins,[5] Bruno was optimistic enough to think that we as a human race were entering into a second Axial Period in universal human consciousness, and Vatican II was evidence of this universal movement happening in Catholic Christianity too.

A NEW LANGUAGE

Part of becoming a world church is being able to express Christianity in new language, breaking out of our Roman-Greek Eurocentric philosophy. As Panikkar put it, "If Christ is to have any meaning for Hindus, Andines, Ibos, Vietnamese, and others who do not belong to the Abrahamic lineage, this meaning can no longer be offered in the garb of Western philosophies."[6] What Bede Griffiths, Abhishiktananda and others asked and are still asking is, can Christianity be interpreted and passed on using the language of Vedanta (late Indian philosophy, based on the Upanishads), for example, or of Mahayana Buddhism, or the language of Taoism or Confucian philosophy? Is it possible to take our experience of the gospel and our tradition and articulate them using other philosophical or mystical language? Bede Griffiths and Abhishik-tananda thought that this may have been the reason for the failure of missionary efforts in the Orient, especially India, because Christianity has used a philosophical language that makes little sense to the Asian mind. We have so often tried to pass on Greek terms and Roman culture (as well as the Roman Rite of the Mass and

[4]Bruno Barnhart, *The Future of Wisdom* (New York: Continuum, 2007), 158–159.
[5]See Ewert Cousins, *Christ of the Twenty-first Century* (New York: Continuum, 1998), 7–10.
[6]Raimon Panikkar, *Christophany: The Fullness of Man,* trans. Alfred DiLascia (Maryknoll, NY: Orbis Books, 2004), 185.

Gregorian chant) instead of allowing the seed of the kerygma to take root in the soil of native philosophical, cultural, and spiritual genius, allowing that the spark of the Divine and the inspiration of the Spirit of God has been at work in other traditions all along.

John Paul II agreed with this in his encyclical *Fides et Ratio*. Yes, in preaching the Gospel, Christianity first encountered Greek philosophy. But this does not mean that other approaches are precluded. "Today," he wrote, "as the Gospel gradually comes into contact with cultural worlds which once lay beyond Christian influence, there are new tasks of inculturation, which means that our generation faces problems not unlike those faced by the Church in the first centuries." And then he says that his thoughts "turn immediately to the lands of the East, so rich in religious and philosophical traditions of great antiquity." Further than that, among these lands, he said that "India has a special place."[7]

Again, we return to the central question: How might another tradition teach me something new about the depth experience of these Persons and energies of the Christian revelation? Or at least teach me a new way to express them. This is particularly poignant in regard to the Third Person, the Spirit, and the corresponding universal energy of spirit within us.

HOVERING AND INDWELLING

What's going on in the cosmos is going on in me. "When I discover *myself* as a unitive energy, welling forth from the darkness of the ground, I have found myself, I am at home," wrote Bruno.[8] Just like the energy itself, so this "welling forth" is important: it's about the complementary energies in the Christian experience. I too am an advocate of this tripartite anthropology, meaning that

---

[7]John Paul II, Encyclical Letter, *Fides et Ratio: On the Relationship between Faith and Reason* (Boston: Pauline Books and Media, 1998), 90–91.

[8]Barnhart *Future of Wisdom*, 90.

the human person is not just body and soul, but spirit, soul, and body, particularly focusing on the use of "spirit" as an *anthropological* element rather than one referring exclusively to God, spirit as an aspect of human being. The boundary between the Person of the Trinity and the energy we share in gets very thin.

There are many understandings of the Holy Spirit, the Third Person of the Trinity in the Christian tradition. What fascinates me most is the way we speak about the Spirit as both an outer reality and an inner reality or, as I like to say, "the Spirit who hovers" and "the Spirit who indwells." Our most popular images of the Holy Spirit are hovering over or descending upon creatures—Jesus at his Baptism, Pentecost—as if God were separate from creation, an interventionist. But from the very beginning there is evidence of another understanding as well.

The second story of creation in the second chapter of Genesis, for example, says that when "the Lord God formed Adam out of clay and blew into his nostrils the breath of life," Adam became a living being. The Kabbalah tradition explains it this way: The main Hebrew term for "soul" is *neshamah*, which means breath. "When the Torah depicts God blowing the breath of life into Adam's nostrils, Adam becomes a 'living being,' a bearer of soul." The Hebrew word is *nepesh*, which is similar to the Arabic word *nafs*. "Our soul comes into being in the moment when God breathes life into us."[9] And we come to understand that that moment is actually *every* moment. God is constantly blowing the breath of life into us. We are being created anew, reborn, in each moment. Rabbi Arthur Green explains it this way:

> *Neshamah* is that breath. It is the place of connection between God and the person, or between the small self of the individual identity and the great Self of being. It is the aspect of us that never separates from our Source, that did not let go of its

[9] Arthur Green, *Ehyeh: A Kabbalah for Tomorrow* (Woodstock, VT: Jewish Lights, 2003), 93.

divine root in the course of that long process of individuation and alienation that we call human life. As difficult as it is to find that place of inner connection to the cosmos and all that is, I believe that it is present within each of us.[10]

This is what I have come to understand "spirit" to be as an element of my being—and I love that this is coming from a Jewish scholar and rabbi, to see it rooted already in the Hebrew scriptures, before Christ. My spirit is the place of connection between God and me. My spirit is the place of connection between the small self of my individual identity and the great Self of Being who is God. My spirit is that aspect of me that has never separated from the Source, that aspect of me that never let go of its divine root in the course of my long process of individuation and alienation that we call human life. My spirit is that place of inner connection to the cosmos and all that is.

Just as there is an apophatic depth to God so there is a fathomless abyss to me where I am already in union with the Great Mother who is Being itself, God who is constantly blowing the breath of life into me, creating me anew, reborn in each moment. Is this why Paul says that if anyone is in Christ there is new creation? (2 Cor. 5:17; Gal. 6:15). Is this why Christian thinkers from Origen to Thomas Aquinas speak about *creatio continua*, continuous creation?

Here's the sacred formula: Breath breathed into mud becomes living being. Spirit + matter = soul. When infused with the Spirit, clay becomes alive; without spirit it is simply clay; *with* spirit it is soul, en-souled, *nepesh*. We find this over and over again in Christian anthropology: spirit, soul, body. The Hebrew mind and the first Christian mind cannot even conceive of a body without soul, or soul without body; they are a substantial unity, given life by the breath of God. But without spirit it is no longer even a body, let alone an ensouled one; it is simply clay.

In the conversation with contemplative prayer and the mystical

---

[10]Ibid.

tradition and popular religiosity there will always be a tension between the inner and outer, the immanent versus the transcendent. I am suggesting, however, that it is the immanent, the experience of the *indwelling* presence of the Spirit of God, that is both our dynamism, our power, and our origin.

St. Paul is not consistent in his use of the Greek term *pneuma* (spirit), and exegetes are often at a loss trying to figure out whether he is referring to the divine *Pneuma*-Spirit or referring to the human spirit-*pneuma* transformed by the grace of the divine *Pneuma* (we can distinguish them in writing with a capital "S" as opposed to a small "s"). Abhishiktananda says, "Paul's intuition boldly soars up to the Real, caring all too little for the fine distinctions of the intellect." But this much seems clear: according to Paul, at the deepest level of *our* spirit is to be found the Spirit of God by which our spirit is quickened, we who "walk not according to the flesh but according to the Spirit" (Rom. 8:14). At the deepest level of *our* interiority there is the interiority of God, the Spirit of God, the Spirit which/who introduces us into the very depths of God. As Paul says in 1 Corinthians: "These things God has revealed to us through the Spirit; for the Spirit searches everything, even the depths of God" (1 Cor. 2:10). Here is Abhishiktananda with an echo of Tillich: "In fact, the Spirit alone can sound and reveal the abyss of Being, for it is in [the Spirit] that the cycle of Being—God's complete self-manifestation in his own mystery—comes to its term."[11]

UNION BY IDENTITY,
UNION BY COMMUNION

As noted earlier, Abhishiktananda, the assumed Indian name of the French Benedictine monk Henri le Saux, and Bede Griffiths, also a Benedictine, from England, were two of the three Western-

---

[11]Abhishiktānanda, *Saccidananda: A Christian Approach to Advaitic Experience*, rev. ed. (Delhi: ISPCK, 1984), 96–97.

ers who co-founded Shantivanam, a Benedictine ashram in South India, and they were as different from each other as night and day. Abhishiktananda was a fiery Breton Frenchman and Bede, for all his orange (*khavi*) robes and asceticism, was always the careful Oxford scholar and poised gentleman.

Abhishiktananda was devoted to the sacred texts of India called the Upanishads and spent a good deal of his later years trying to reconcile his Christian faith with the experience of *advaita* as taught by the Vedanta school of Indian philosophy and spirituality. Put simply, the basic intuition of the Upanishads and Vedanta is that Ultimate Reality and the individual creature are "not two." That's the literal meaning of the Sanskrit word *a-dvaita*—"not two." And the individual self ultimately, when it reaches spiritual perfection, disappears into the Great Self "like a drop into the ocean," as the famous maxim goes. I call this *union* (with God) *by identity*. So a good Hindu of this school can say, "*Aham Brahmāsmi*—I am God," meaning not that I, Cyprian, am God, but that Cyprian has dissolved and there is only God-*Brahman,* the ground of being. Like our word "spirit" with a capital "S" and a small "s," so with the Sanskrit word *atman:* it can be understood as either the divine Ground of consciousness or the individual self. So there is the *jivātman*–the individual self/ground of consciousness, and there is *Parātman*–the Great Self, who is the ultimate ground and source of all consciousness. When I make the interior journey, the *telos,* the ultimate goal is to discover that the ground of my consciousness is none other than the Ground of Being. Another of the *mahāvākyas* or the "great sayings" of India (like *Aham Brahmāsmi*) is *Ayam Atma Brahma*—"The Self is Brahman."[12] The ground of my own self and the Ground of all Being are "not-two." My individual self has disappeared into the Great Self like a drop into the ocean. This is an expression of a subtle but ground-shifting spiritual experience.

Bede Griffiths, however, was a great lover of another Indian

---

[12] The other two classical *mahāvākyas*–great sayings are *Tat tvam asi*—"Thou art that" and *So'ham*–"I am that One."

scripture, the *Bhagavad Gita*, which teaches about the way of union through the various types of yoga. Bede felt that Abhishiktananda at times went too far in overstressing *advaita*, and he stressed more the way of love, what I call *union* (with God) *by communion*. This is much more typical of the Christian expression of the mystical end such as found in the bridal mysticism of Bernard of Clairvaux and the Carmelites. Bede taught that the mystery of communion in God and with God is that "the Father and the Son become a total unity and are yet distinct," and that is true of human beings and God as well: "We are one, and yet we are distinct. There is never a total loss of self." Even if in consciousness there could be, or could seem to be, pure identity, "in love there's never pure identity because love involves two," he says, "and yet the two become one. That's the great mystery." Therefore, Bede thought that the Indian metaphor of the ocean and the droplet that re-merges with the ocean was not quite adequate. You could say the drop merges in the ocean, but you could also say the ocean is present in the drop: "In the ultimate state the individual is totally there, totally realized, but also in total communion with all the rest."[13]

Scholars of the Christian mystical tradition often attempt to describe these two different understandings of mystical experience, one as "literal identity, where the mystic loses all sense of [self] and is absorbed into God," and the other as "the union that is experienced as the consummation of love, in which the lover and the beloved remain intensely aware both of themselves and of the other."[14] Another way to put it is to identify on the one hand mysticism of the sacraments and a Christocentric spirituality based on both sacred and secular imagery, especially the "bridal mysticism" of women religious in Flanders, France, Holland, and the Rhineland, as compared with the "mysticism of being" of Meister Eckhart and his lineage, which includes Johannes Tauler, Henri

---

[13]Bede Griffiths quoted in Rene Weber, *Dialogues with Saints and Sages* (London: Routledge and Kegan Paul, 1986), 171–172.

[14]Andrew Louth, *The Origins of the Christian Mystical Tradition: From Plato to Denys* (Oxford: Clarendon Press, 1981), xv.

Suso, Jan van Ruusbroec, and the English mystics Richard Rolle, Walter Hilton, and Julian of Norwich. This mysticism of being is a total stripping of self; it "aims to transcend images and enter into the 'darkness' and the 'nothingness' of the Godhead," leading the soul to shed all that is "superfluous, contrary or unequal" to God's most essential Being. In other words, an apophatic anthropology and spirituality: self has dissolved and there is only God.[15] It is this latter which is the lesser known in Christianity, but one we are aiming at bringing more to the fore.

These views—*union by identity* and *union by communion*—don't have to be mutually exclusive but actually are the fundamental complementary energies in the Christian experience, Baptismal and Eucharistic. Union by identity is one way to express and explain the Baptismal experience and the unfolding of that experience, basking in the experience that "God's love has been poured into our hearts through the Holy Spirit that has been given to us" (Rom. 5:5) and, especially, "It is no longer I who live, it is Christ who lives in me" (see Gal. 2:20). Then there is the Eucharistic energy, which is union by communion, communion not just with *God* but with one another, our being broken and poured out for the sake of the world. This is the Eucharist of the washing of the feet as much as if not more than the Eucharist of the sacred species, the Eucharistic energy of *Ite missa est*—"Go in peace, glorifying God by your life," our being broken up and poured out like the bread and wine. This is that same love of God now "pouring out of the believer's heart like a stream of life-giving water" (Jn. 7:39). So there are two energies—the Baptismal energy of union by identity and the Eucharistic energy of union by communion. Embracing and exploring the depths of both of these are pivotal for a rearticulation of Christian spirituality, since I am not sure we truly understand either the depth experience of union with God by the indwelling presence or the energy that that immanence gives us for our being

---

[15]Oliver Davies, *God Within: The Mystical Tradition of Northern Europe* (New York: Paulist Press, 1988), 2–4.

and action in the world. Bruno calls it "participatory consciousness," as First Peter describes it, "that you may be participants in the divine nature" (1 Pt. 2:4).

And this is the Third Movement, the energy of Spirit in our spirit, and the beginning of our participation in Divinity, and consciousness of that participation. Here Bruno writes almost breathlessly of

> the dimension of dynamism, of energy, of movement, relationship, communion, personal experience, human freedom and creativity, the world of *psyche* and of the feminine. It is the principle of development, whether within the individual person, in human history, or in the evolution of the cosmos. We are always on the threshold of a great renaissance, an "Age of the Spirit." . . . We experience the dawn of this new age in a hundred ways—related to the Spirit, to psyche, to the emerging feminine, to poetry, art, and music.[16]

SHEKINAH

After the close of the Jewish biblical canon, in the rabbinic tradition and particularly in the medieval Kabbalah, the Spirit of God came to be spoken of as *shekinah.* The use of this name for the Divine has also seen a resurgence in Jewish congregations and settings over the last half-century.

Shekinah is a grammatically feminine word that comes from the Hebrew verb *shakhan,* which means "to dwell," and it is used in several texts that speak of God dwelling among the people: for example, Exodus 25:8—"And have them make me a sanctuary, so that I may dwell among them"; and Exodus 29:45–46—"I will dwell among the Israelites, and I will be their God. And they shall know that I am the Lord their God, who brought them out of the

---

[16]Barnhart, *Future of Wisdom,* 6.

land of Egypt that I might dwell among them." Instead of saying that God or God's Spirit descends onto the Holy of Holies, the rabbis would say that the *shekinah* filled the Temple.

What does this matter to those who call themselves Christian? When we hear of Jesus "filled with the Holy Spirit," we should think of this *shekinah*, filling the temple of his body.[17] The *shekinah* rests between two people who sit together and speak the words of the Torah, and we ought to think of this when Jesus says, "When two or three are together in my name, there am I in their midst" (Mt. 18:20). This is important because here, as we saw in the Catechism, is the quality of God's immanence, God's manifestation to humanity in nearness as opposed to transcendence.

Catholic theologian Elisabeth Schüssler-Fiorenza points out that the *shekinah* is also associated with divine compassion: "When the people are brought low, the Shekinah lies in the dust, anguished by human suffering," and she quotes a saying from the Mishnah concerning capital punishment: "When a human being suffers, what does the shekinah say? My head is too heavy for Me, My arm is too heavy for Me. And if God is so grieved over the blood of the wicked that is shed, how much more so over the blood of the righteous." For Schüssler-Fiorenza, *shekinah* isn't just a "feminine dimension of God"; this is God as She-Who-Dwells-Within, the "divine presence in compassionate engagement with the conflictual world, source of vitality and consolation in the struggle."[18]

Not to deny the inspired image of the Spirit as a descending dove, which we find in the Christian scriptures, but here again is evidence of other imagery for the Holy Spirit—fire, water, wind. The point about the Jewish mindset not being a philosophical one but a mythical one comes here again, because ancient Jewish

---

[17]See the readings for Monday, 5th week of Ordinary Time, year II in the Universal Lectionary.

[18]Elisabeth Schüssler-Fiorenza, *In Memory of Her* (New York: Crossroads, 1983), 85–86. See also Elizabeth A. Johnson's excellent treatment of this theme in *Women, Earth, and Creator Spirit* (New York: Paulist Press, 1993), 51–56.

Christianity too "did not express itself in Greek discursive termi-
nology, but in Semitic metaphorical language … in images, not
in logical concepts."[19]

There is a lot of evidence that the first Christians, all of whom
were Jewish, used to speak of the Holy Spirit as feminine—asso-
ciating her either with Sophia or with *shekinah*. This is partly due
to the fact that the Hebrew word for "spirit," *ruach*, is feminine in
nearly all cases. So are the Aramaic and Syrian words for "spirit,"
rucha, but it's not just about language and the gender of words.

There are various sources in early Christianity that associate
the Holy Spirit with Sophia. The *Homilies* of so-called Pseudo-
Clementine (written under the name of the bishop and martyr
Clement of Rome) tells us that "Peter says, 'One is He who said
to His Wisdom, "Let us make a man."' His *Sophia*, with Her He
Himself always rejoiced just as with His own *pneumati* [spirit]."
Theophilus of Antioch (in *Against Autolycus*) writes, "God made
everything through his Logos and Sophia"—and then he appropri-
ates Psalm 33:6 to read—"for by His *Logos* the heavens were made
firm and by His Spirit all their power." Irenaeus of Lyons in *Against
Heretics* mentions "the Son and the Holy Spirit, the Word and the
Wisdom," writing in Latin, *Spiritus* and *Sapientia*; and again, in
another place, "For with Him were always present the Word and
the Wisdom, the Son and the Spirit." Epiphanius, the bishop of
Salamis, and the great Hippolytus of Rome both cite a prophet
named Elxai, whose writings are lost to us now, who "describes
Christ as a kind of power . . . and the Holy Spirit is said to be
like Christ too, but She is a female being." And both Origen and
Jerome several times mention one particular phrase from the now
lost Gospel of the Hebrews, which appears to have been in use
among the first Jewish Christians, originally composed in Aramaic:
Jesus himself saying, "My mother"—the Greek word used there

---

[19]Johannes van Oort, "The Holy Spirit as Feminine: Early Christian Testimonies
and Their Interpretation," *HTS Theological Studies* 72, no. 1 (Pretoria 2016): 4.

is *mētēr*—"My mother, the Holy Spirit, took me just now by one of my hairs and carried me off to the great Mount Tabor." Origen says concerning this passage that "if one accepts that, one could see who Jesus' *mētēr*-mother is."[20]

INNER AND OUTER SPIRIT

It is primary for Christians to understand the Holy Spirit as the Third Person of the Trinity. For us God is relationship, and we focus primarily on the relationship of Jesus and the Father. And the Holy Spirit *is* the relationship between Jesus and the Father, the love, the song they sing to each other. This passage from the Czech writer Maria Popova concerning relationships in general applies very well here. No relationship is ever only between two people, she writes, but between three, the two partners, "each with their pre-existing patterns of love and loss, and the third presence of the relationship itself—an intersubjective co-creation that becomes the third partner, endowed with the power to deepen those patterns, or to change them."[21] This love between the First Person and the Second, between the Source and the Wisdom, is so powerful that we speak of it as its own Person, its own constellation of energy. Remember again what we learned from Panikkar, that "person" encompasses a whole complex web of relationships. An "I" is a *person* only to the extent that it is not isolated. And this love between the First and the Second Person itself is a force, a personality, an intentionality, as love always is a creative force, in marriages, loves, friendships: love is procreative. It brings forth an intersubjective co-creation that becomes the third partner.

Of course, even before the Christian dispensation, before the

---

[20]Much of this is dependent on the work of van Oort, "The Holy Spirit as Feminine."

[21]Maria Popova, The Marginalian.org, October 24, 2021.

historical Jesus was born, there was the Holy Spirit who was with the Word and Wisdom. What does God do? God speaks. This is the Word, the second person of the Trinity, as we already saw in Psalm 36: "God spoke and it came to be; God commanded, it sprang into being." Everything sprang into being because this Word and Wisdom too was/is filled with God's Spirit, God's energy. We might say that the Word gives form, shape, and intentionality to the energy of the Spirit. On the other hand, God's Word is powerful precisely because it is filled with God's energy, God's Spirit.

And then a new portion of the Spirit was poured out at Pentecost, the Spirit of the Risen Jesus. Helpfully, the ninth-century theologian John Scotus Eriugena distinguished between what he calls the *datum*, the spirit that is already given in creation and ongoing creation and the inherent *imago Dei*, and the *donum*, the gifts of the new creation, the gift of the Christ event, the new portion of the Spirit written about so often by Saint Paul. We find this also in Clement of Alexandria where he distinguishes between "the spiritual principle received at creation" and "the distinctive characteristic of the Holy Spirit, which comes to us through faith."[22]

I want to highlight the *datum*, placing the accent on the truth that God is already present in creation in some marvelous way, breathed into the clay, even before the gift of the Holy Spirit given at Pentecost and through the sacraments. Biblical revelation tells us that in the human person there is a breath, a spark of the Divine, if you will, already in all people. That latter image, the "spark of the Divine," tends to be a mistrusted and disputed image, worrying that there is a suggestion that God would be divided into parts. But the breath image stays strong, particularly if we think God is constantly blowing the breath of life into us, not just once at creation. This is the basis for our yearning for self-transcendence—what Karl Rahner called the supernatural existential. Our deepest

---

[22] *Stromateis*, 6.16.134.2, see John Behr, *Asceticism and Anthropology in Irenaeus and Clement* (New York: Oxford University Press, 2000), 137.

self is this breath, that spark, the *imago Dei* given in creation and ongoing creation.

But for a moment let's talk about the *donum*—that new portion of the Spirit, the distinctive characteristic of the Holy Spirit, which comes to us through faith.

POURED INTO OUR HEARTS

The most common image we have for Pentecost is that of the Holy Spirit coming down upon the heads of the apostles, and therefore by extension pouring over the whole church. The liturgical readings for the feast emphasize that "I will pour out my spirit on all flesh" from the prophet Joel (see 3:1–5) and also emphasize the "noise like a strong driving wind" and the tongues of fire that came to rest on the apostles that we hear from the Acts of the Apostles (see 2:1–11).

But there is another set of liturgical readings for that feast: the Vigil Mass can be celebrated the evening before. The Vigil Mass starts out with the entrance antiphon from Paul's letter to the Romans: "The love of God is poured into our hearts by the Spirit living in us" (5:5). And we hear, also from Romans, how the Spirit prays in us "with sighs too deep for words" (see 8:22–27); and from the Gospel of John, Jesus crying out that "Out of the believer's heart shall flow rivers of living water," which John tells us he said "about the Spirit which believers in him were to receive" (7:37–39). In other words, the Spirit does not just intervene from above and cover us; the Spirit is poured into our hearts and pulses through our veins.

This also is what Pentecost is all about—the Holy Spirit living *in* us, and that same Spirit then pouring out of us like a stream of life-giving water. The Holy Spirit dwells in us as the power and the energy of God. All of Easter—indeed the life, passion, death, resurrection, and ascension of Jesus—have been pointing toward this, our own spiritual rebirth, from individuals to persons, a regenerate humanity, new creation. We are the reason this has all happened. And that ties it together: this is the immanent Spirit, the *shekinah* who dwells in me, a Mother who continually brings me to birth—a *creatio continua*.

10

Dynamic Energy

The fourteenth-century Byzantine hesychast theologian Gregory Palamas distinguished between God's essence and God's energy. We cannot know God's essence, the hesychasts taught, and we are not consubstantial (of one substance) with God in the same way that the great councils of the church say Jesus was, the famous *homoousias*. We can, however, know God's energy, which Gregory and his friends call the "uncreated energies" of God, and which are at work in us. These are supernatural in the sense that they come from beyond the body and its senses; they are not *natural* to the body and its senses. They also aren't merely mental and intellectual powers of the mind or soul. This power comes from beyond all that, beyond our bodies, beyond our souls. This strikes me as resonant with the Kabbalah notion of *shekinah*, except now we are talking about filling the temple of *our* body.

At the same time, even though they are not natural to us, by virtue of our spirit we can *participate* in this uncreated energy of God. It can flow through us. As a matter of fact, this is our right by Baptism! Gregory Palamas and his friends in the East truly believed that our intelligence *and* our senses, our souls *and* our bodies, could be, should be, are meant to be, transformed by grace, a transformative experience that would lead us to that supreme end for which we were created: realization of our union with God.

The two different ways of knowing that we normally operate with are through our senses and through our intellect. But Gregory says that if we have not just the power of our senses and intellect but have also "attained spiritual and supernatural grace," we can know "*spiritually*, above sense and intelligence, that God is Spirit, for in our entirety we become God, and know God in God."[1]

He was not the first or the only one to use that shocking phrase, by the way—that "we become God." Basil the Great, for example, is quoted saying so in the Office of Readings, the official liturgy of the Church, on Tuesday of the Seventh Week of Easter. And he too is specifically referring to the Spirit, from his "Treatise on the Holy Spirit": "Through the Spirit we acquire a likeness to God; indeed we attain what is beyond our most sublime aspirations—we become God."[2] This is what it means to be deified, to become God by participation, and this may be our version of India's intuition about "union by identity."

Our created faculties, the abilities of our body and even of our soul with its mind and its whole spectrum of consciousness, are not enough for us to see God. To see God, we need God's own peculiar power, God's life and God's energy. In other words, we need grace. And this is what we believe Jesus did in his person: he united human energy with divine energy, enabling human beings to be in union with God.[3] In Jesus, because of the Christ event, we believe that a new portion of grace was poured out on the human race.

Another important point about Gregory's teaching, especially for a truly integral view, is Gregory's stress on the surpassing dignity of the human body and not just that of the rational soul. This was a great breakthrough for someone like Gregory Palamas who would have been so deeply influenced by Neo-Platonism and

---

[1] Tr. II, 3, 31. John Meyendorff, *A Study of Gregory Palamas* (London: Faith Press, 1964), 172.

[2] *Office of Readings*, Tuesday, Seventh Week of Easter, 632.

[3] Meyendorff, *Gregory Palamas*, 173.

its idea that the "body is a tomb for the soul."[4] Even though this divine energy comes from a supernatural source, a source beyond body and soul, neither the body nor the soul are left behind. And not only the soul but even the body has the capacity to show forth the glory and beauty of God; both body and soul are transformed by this divinization. This is why the Transfiguration has remained such an icon particularly for Eastern monasticism. As a matter of fact, the transformative divine light sometimes continues to be manifest in the bodies of some saints even after their death, hence the veneration of relics and tombs of the saints.

DIVINE MADNESS

Speaking of bodies, perhaps the best language we really have for this in the West is the Greek notion of *eros*. One of our best contemporary spiritual writers, Ronald Rolheiser, has a beautiful treatment of this theme, using Goethe's phrase the "holy longing" in his book of the same name. He says *eros* is "an unquenchable fire, a restlessness, a longing, a disquiet, a hunger, a loneliness, a gnawing nostalgia, a wildness that cannot be tamed, a congenital all-embracing ache that lies at the center of human experience and is the ultimate force that drives everything else."[5]

Rolheiser insists, and I agree, that our contemporary search to define Christian spirituality has to be rooted in *eros*. Christian spirituality isn't an uprooting of desire (as the Buddhists might say); it's about what we *do* with desire. Our spirituality "takes root in the eros inside of us and it is all about how we shape and discipline that eros." Shaping and disciplining our natural energies is the real goal of asceticism, not suppressing or punishing. *Eros* "is soul and soul gives energy," carrying with it not only desire, disquiet, nostalgia,

[4]William Johnston, *Mystical Theology: The Science of Love* (Maryknoll, NY: Orbis Books, 1998), 81.

[5]Ronald Rolheiser, *The Holy Longing: The Search for a Christian Spirituality* (New York: Doubleday, 1999), 4.

lust, and appetite, but also hope and energy. The Greeks say that we are fired into life with a madness that is the root of all love, hate, creativity, joy, and sadness. Christians should agree with that, and we add that God has put that madness inside us, so that we might share in God's work of creation, and ultimately contemplate that which we have helped create and burst with a joy and "swell in a delight that breaks the prison of [our] selfishness,"[6] our autonomy, the independence which we cling to.

And for this reason, our sexual energy too lies at the center of the spiritual life and is itself a manifestation of divine energy. Indeed a healthy sexuality (and that word "healthy" is an important caveat, a check on libertinism) "is the single most powerful vehicle there is to lead us to selflessness and joy, just as unhealthy sexuality helps constellate selfishness and unhappiness as does nothing else."[7] A healthy spirituality trains that madness to be a friend, hope, and energy—rather than a distraction.

Could it be that traditions that have intuited something about a divine power with which we are fired into life, a divine "madness" that is the root of all love and creativity—such as the Chinese notion of *chi*, the Hindu *kundalini*, or the Greek *eros*—have a Christian equivalent? Can we come to recognize that God has put this energy inside us so that we might become participants in the divine nature?

RETURN TO THE MOTHER

This is what I have come to understand my "spirit" to be: the place of connection between God and me, the place of connection between the small self of my individual identity and the great Self of Being, that aspect of me that has never separated from the Source, that aspect of me that never let go of its divine root in the

---

[6] Ibid., 193.
[7] Ibid.

course of my long process of individuation and alienation that we call human life, that place of inner connection to the cosmos and all that is.

The problem is that we are out of touch with that deepest aspect of our being and so out of touch with the divine Spirit and the energy that pours forth from it and Her. There's hope though. In order to fulfill our humanness to the highest degree, or to use the images we began this journey with, in order to move from individual to person, we need to recover the dynamic power of the ground, the Ground of Being, which, let me add, is also the ground of consciousness. And we have to go back to the Great Mother to do so.

However, the return to the Mother, recovering the dynamic ground, is going to be experienced as a kind of death, dying to our stubborn insistence on our autonomy and independence, a death to the individual that gives birth to the person, a sacrifice of our independence to move into relationship and interdependence. The Christian understanding of the Paschal Mystery—Jesus' life, passion, death, resurrection, and the coming of the Holy Spirit—can now be seen anew, as a powerful and universal icon of this entire process. Jesus' descent into the tomb becomes a return to the womb of new birth, and this is our Baptismal experience, our immersion in Jesus' death and resurrection, and the beginning of new life in Christ. In the *reditus*—the "return to the One" of the Greek philosophers, or in the soul's interior ascent to God in contemplative enstasy, in the *samadhi*-absorption of the *rishis*, the Buddhists, and the Taoist hermits, this sense of distinct identity disappears into the Great Mother like a drop into the ocean. But for Christians, our belief in the Resurrection tells us that it is at this point that "the human person awakens to the non-dual divine light as one's own identity," and that awakening consequently leads us to experience "the divine power within oneself as one's own generative freedom, the capability of creating a human world."[8]

---

[8]Bruno Barnhart, *The Future of Wisdom* (New York: Continuum, 2007), 143.

There's a marvelous equivalent of this in the Sufi tradition called *fanā*. *Fanā* is normally translated as "annihilation" of the self, but it is not to be understood in the sense that someone or something from the outside is annihilating us. It is more like a gradual dissipation of the individual self. This is a common theme in the poetry of Rumi, for instance. A common practice in Sufi circles that goes with this concept is that of *zhikr*, which is translated as "remembrance." Zhikr is basically the repetitive chanting of litanies and names of God derived from the Qur'an and taught by the *murshid*-teacher/guide to the student. This is done in a way that leads to an almost trance-like state, until "self is forgotten and God is remembered," as my friends explain it.[9] What is said about zhikr could apply very well to Christian prayer and meditation; we pray until self is forgotten and God is remembered.

One of my friends who is steeped in the Sufi tradition wrote me a beautiful description of how this plays out in ordinary life as well.

All of life offers us opportunities to experience and practice fanā. In the grief of losing a loved one, a relationship, or even a calling, we feel a part of our being annihilated. That which once was, is no longer. . . . There are always parts of us, ego constructs, that are ripe for dying. When we can release them with love, something greater and, dare I say, more holy is waiting to emerge. Think of a caterpillar who must liquefy in order to turn into a butterfly, a seed that must break open to become a tree, a heart that must be broken open to allow the Divine in.[10]

From the Christian point of view, how many different ways does Jesus remind us that "those who want to save their life will lose it,

---

[9]There is also *fanā-fi shieik* and *fanā-fi-Pir*—being attuned to one's personal teacher or the leader of one's particular order or even someone with whom one feels affinity; *fanā-fi-Rasul*— attuning to the Prophet or another master or saint; and ultimately *fanā-fi-Allah*— attuning to the True Beloved, God beyond concepts, names or forms.

[10]Thanks to Gitanjali Lori Rivera for these thoughts.

and those who lose their life for my sake will find it"? (Mt. 16:25).
When one is adequately mature psychologically and emotionally
(a common saying in formation work in religious life is "You have
to have a self before you can give yourself away"), there are two
aspects of this what I call "self-naughting" that Christianity focuses
on. On the one hand, there are countless little acts of going against
our unchecked appetites and engrained behaviors, even something
as small as a pause to offer a prayer of thanks before wolfing down
a meal, taking a breath before an impatient, unkind word rolls
off the tongue, and making sure that we are the masters over our
tastes for even legitimate pleasures such as entertainment, alcohol,
or sexual activity instead of them ruling us. This is the beginning
level of asceticism even before such extraordinary practices such
as fasting and celibate chastity. A positive practice of fanā is also
simply found in service. "No one has greater love than this," Jesus
teaches his disciples, than "to lay down one's life for one's friends"
(Jn. 15:13) just after he washes their feet. St. Benedict in his *Rule*
for monks calls this "mutual obedience": all are to pursue not what
they judge best for themselves, but instead what they judge best
for someone else. There are many ways we can, as our Sufi friends
say, "die before we die."[11]

But it doesn't end there, and this is the point: the spiritual annihilation of *fanā* is followed by a phenomenon known as *baqā*,
which means revival, a re-vivification, and a return to the self, but a
return to an *enhanced* self. As my friend wrote, "Walking through a
burnt forest, one can experience fanā and baqā simultaneously. We
see the death of the old trees and the sprouting of new growth in
that same tree." Union with God (or our reunion with the Mother)
and our so-called annihilation, does not destroy our natural ca-
pacities, but fulfills them! Like Antony emerging from the tomb,
divinized. When the obscuring egoism of our autonomy has been
stripped away, we discover the divine presence at the heart of our
own being, *as* the heart of our being, and from this we experience

---

[11]See Benedict's *Rule*, chapter 71. Translation my own.

greater self-realization and *greater* self-control. In this revival, as in resurrection, we come bounding back more fully human, with the ideal humanness that God intended all along. The realization of our union with God—the Baptismal energy—becomes the fount of life-giving water, dynamism, the source of our going out of ourselves in participation—the Eucharistic energy. This could be specifically Christianity's contribution to the conversation. Bruno thought that *this* is Christ's basic gift to humanity: freedom and generativity based on the knowledge of our rootedness in Being itself who is God.

This is when we really move from individual to person. The self doesn't disappear like a drop into the ocean, but instead comes bursting forth from this "death" to move forward again with spiritual dynamism and a relationship with the body and the earth recovered. And we evolve now *beyond* person—not pre-personal but *trans*-personal, to communion with others, with nature, with God.[12] Because this is not just our own dynamic ground: this is the dynamic ground of *everything* because it is Being itself. As we know from Thomas Aquinas all the way to Paul Tillich, God is not *a* being—God is Being itself. So along with *us* being a new creation, the Scriptures dream of "a new heaven and a new earth," (Is. 65:17, 66:22, 1 Pt. 3:13, Rev. 21:21)—all that shares Being. To paraphrase St. Paul, all creation is groaning and in agony while we work this out, this redemption of our bodies. Or as Teilhard would tell us, not union with creation, nor simply union with God, but union with God through creation, a new heaven and a new earth. The new creation begins with the human person and catalyzes a rebirth of all creation. This is the priesthood of the human person. Our spirit is that place of inner connection to the cosmos and all that is. We could say this simple prayer drawn from the Big Book of Alcoholics Anonymous: "Relieve me of the bondage of self that I may better do Your will."

---

[12] This, by the way, is why Washburn's school of psychology is called "Transpersonal."

INSCENDENCE

How do we recover this lost, forgotten energy?

Here I want to bring in Thomas Berry's notion of what he calls *inscendence*, further elucidated by the depth psychologist and wilderness guide Bill Plotkin. "Inscendence," that is, as opposed to "transcendence." Whereas transcendence is our drive *away* from the world, *away* from creation, *away* from our bodies, inscendence is the movement within, the inward movement that is needed to complement and indeed correct our transcendence.

We begin with the assumption that our cultures are insufficient to offer any solutions to the problems we face in the twenty-first century, because they are distorted and have lost their integrity.[13] How and why did this happen? Berry and Plotkin would point toward a "radical anthropocentrism" (meaning that everything centers around the human being) that "rejects our role as an integral member of the earth community."[14] That exaggerated anthropocentrism itself is rooted in an overemphasis on a transcendent God as opposed to an indwelling and pervading sense of the Divine, and consequently an overemphasis on the belief that our destiny is in another world "with God" who is detached from creation. And that, of course, tends to desacralize the phenomenal world and not recognize the symbiotic relationship that human beings have with creation.[15] And so we can "pave paradise and put up a parking lot" because our real home is somewhere else. But the truth is that we are a *part* of creation; as Fr. Bede would say, human beings are creation coming into consciousness. We human beings, with our reflexive consciousness, are that reality in whom the entire Earth

---

[13]Thomas Berry, *The Dream of the Earth* (San Francisco: Sierra Club Books, 1990), 208.

[14]Ibid.

[15]Bill Plotkin, "Inscendence—The Key to the Great Work of Our Time," in *Thomas Berry, Dreamer of the Earth: The Spiritual Ecology of the Father of Environmentalism*, ed. Ervin Laszlo and Allan Combs (Rochester, VT: Inner Traditions, 2011), 49.

itself comes to a special mode of reflexive consciousness. "We ourselves are a mystical quality of the Earth,"[16] profoundly united with every creature.

The problem is, as I have been pointing out thus far, we have lost touch with this depth of our own consciousness, especially the mystical dimension of ourselves. Our cultures have lost their integrity because we human beings who make up society and culture have lost *our* integrity.

Here Berry would agree with Albert Einstein that "no problem can be solved from the same consciousness that created it." The problems that we face as a human race today are not going to be solved by the same way of thinking that created those problems in the first place! We need a new consciousness, an evolved way of thinking. Berry cites the Nobel Prize–winning German physician and scientist Paul Ehrlich, who suggested that what we need is a "quasi-religious transformation of contemporary cultures."[17] I would nuance that by saying that we need a transformation that can come about only by the inner work of spirituality, because it is the Spirit, at the point of *our* spirit, that is the only real engine of that transformation. As Saint Paul wrote in the Letter to the Romans, we need to *not be conformed to this world but transformed by the renewal of our minds* (Rom. 12:12). The Greek word Paul uses there for "mind" is *nous*, a very specific concept that cannot be reduced to "mind" as we normally understand it, certainly not just the rational mind, and this is why I always prefer the broader term "consciousness." We need to be transformed by the renewal of our consciousness. And this can happen only at a depth we rarely access.

Beneath our rationality, deeper than our rationality, there is a numinous dimension to our own consciousness, a part of our own selves that still remembers our primal imperative before it was covered over and distorted by our cultural coding and before we

[16]Ibid., 47.
[17]Berry, *The Dream of the Earth*, 207.

forgot our Source, the Font of our Being, the Great Mother, in our journey outward toward the world of discovery. This is the genius divinely embedded in our very DNA, our "genetic imperative." However, it isn't merely a physical endowment; it is our richest psychic spiritual endowment as well, "our guiding and inspiring force."[18] The physicality of all this in Berry's writing is important and not just as a metaphor. It's a firm belief that encoded in our DNA is the soul's code, the law written on our hearts, if you will, and the spiritual power that has been the thrust behind our evolution, in consciousness and otherwise, from micro to macro, all along. Our *genetic* coding, that is, as opposed to our *cultural* coding. Even our cultural coding has to get stripped away too at some point, maybe especially: *Here there is no slave or free, no Jew or Greek, no woman or man* (Gal. 3:28). So if we are to be "reinvented," it is to make us what we have been or have been meant to be all along that perhaps got covered over or distorted by our cultural coding.

And inscendence happens when human consciousness makes the interior journey and comes into contact with, and is transformed by, this depth dimension of our consciousness, a "mystery beyond its ken,"[19] but which is also the deepest part of ourselves, our own fathomless depth. There are times in our life when, as individuals, we have to "descend to our instinctive resources in order to reinvent ourselves." The bigger issue that Berry and Plotkin are both addressing is that "there are times when our species, collectively, must do so" also, and this is such an era.[20] So this is work on ourselves that we human beings are doing for all creation which is groaning and in agony while we work out this redemption of our bodies.

If we truly believe that the Word and Wisdom of God are the intentionality behind creation, then we must recognize that we share this numinous dimension with creation itself. Again, our spirit is that place of inner connection to the cosmos and all that

---

[18]Ibid., 208.
[19]Plotkin, "Inscendence," 46.
[20]Ibid., 49.

is. As Pope Francis prays in *Laudati Si'*, we need to "discover the worth of each thing, to be filled with awe and contemplation, to recognize that we are profoundly united with every creature as we journey towards your infinite light."[21] For this reason, the wisdom we seek will "sprout from the depths of the human psyche" as well as "from our encounters with the mysteries of the natural world."[22] With Antony, the father of monks, our book will be the book of nature. Here we have resonances with the Stoic understanding of the *logos*, who is both like a fire that permeates all of creation and the highest realm of our own consciousness. This passage from Marcus Aurelius's *Meditations* is particularly sublime, explaining the *logos* as the unifying ground.

> Everything is interwoven, and the web is holy;
> none of its parts are unconnected.
> They are composed harmoniously,
> and together they compose the world.
> One world, made up of all things.
> One divinity, present in them all.
> One substance and one law—the *logos* that all rational
>   beings share.
> And one truth . . . the culmination of one process,
> beings who share the same birth, the same *logos*.[23]

Since we share this numinous dimension with creation itself, the nature-based traditions, the primal traditions, and the tribal peoples have a precious gift for us now, to teach us how to make this inward journey through and with creation, because they not only understand that to remain viable we have to live in such a way that is beneficial both for our species and our surrounding community (i.e., nature), they also value this sense of the pervading divine spirit. The Christian ascetical tradition already has common

[21]Pope Francis, *Laudato Si'* (2015), www.vatican.va.
[22]Plotkin, 42.
[23]Marcus Aurelius, *Meditations,* book 7, no. 9, 98–99.

ground with cultures from all times and places that have invented rituals and practices that help their members who are developmentally ready to descend to this depth of soul, what I am calling our spirit. We are speaking here of consciousness-shifting technologies such as fasting and extended periods of silence and solitude, the *samā* and *zhikr* (dance and chanting the Beautiful Names of God) of the Sufi tradition, as well as ceremonial sweats, breathwork, meditation and yoga, even extreme physical exertion.[24] This shifts the tone of asceticism from penitential and punitive to its root in Greek mysticism, more like an athletic training that makes the spiritual journey through, with, and in the body rather than an attempt to cast it off.

Plotkin laments that in contemporary Western cultures "we live as if the spiritual descent is no longer necessary." Whereas ancient myths are trying to tell us "that we each must undertake the journey of descent if we are to heal ourselves at the deepest levels and reach a full and authentic adulthood."[25] (See Richard Rohr's brilliant work around male rites of initiation in this regard as well.) It hardly has to be pointed out that Jesus in the desert and Jesus in the tomb are poignant images to describe this inscendence, as poignant as any ancient myths, a sinking back into the Source of everything to be remade on the third day. This is also a good description of what we are being asked to do during Lent, for example: the forty days in the desert, stripping down to basics, just as in the ascetical life in general. Even further, this is also as good a description as any of what must happen in every life at some decisive point in the spiritual journey, when we are developmentally ready: we must be reinvented, regenerated, "born again" by the deconstruction of our false self, our mask, our persona, and make the journey down to the core of our being.

This is also the beauty of the practice and the naked scope of

[24]Plotkin, "Inscendence," 51.
[25]Bill Plotkin, *Soulcraft: Crossing into the Mysteries of Nature and Psyche* (Novato, CA: New World Library, 2003), 11–12.

contemplative prayer, of meditation and yoga, that we sink into our own bodily-ness to discover that which is deeper than—and the source of—material reality and our intellectual power, the ground of our being and the ground of all consciousness. As William Johnston wrote, in the purified tranquility of darkness, "the soul goes down, down to the very center of its own being, nakedly to encounter God who secretly dwells in silent love at the sovereign point of the spirit."[26]

FULL PERSONHOOD

If we want to reach our full personhood, at some point we need to return to the mother—as Jesus tells Nicodemus to be born again—return to the Great Mother who is the source of our dynamism and recover what we left behind. But this return to the womb is going to feel like a death, an entry into great darkness, because it will mean the death of our independence, a death to our autonomy, the death of our individuality—though the birth of our person! And Washburn too says that the best example of that return is Jesus' death and descent into the tomb. It was a return to the Mother, a return to Mother Earth, a return to the womb of new creation. And so the scripture readings we hear from First Peter during the Easter season speak of a "new birth to living hope, and how like newborn children we should thirst for the pure spiritual milk" (see 1:3–9 and 2:2).

We could pray with this poem of Rumi:

Dissolver of sugar, dissolve me,
if this is the time.
Do it gently with a touch of a hand, or a look.
Every morning I wait at dawn. That's when

---

[26]William Johnston, *The Mysticism of the Cloud of Unknowing* (New York: Desclee, 1967), 186.

it's happened before. Or do it suddenly
like an execution. How else
can I get ready for death?[27]

As we end our meditation on the Third Person of the Trinity and the accompanying energy, these words of John Main so simply summarize what we have been about: "What we have to learn to do is take our potentiality absolutely seriously to understand that the Spirit of the One who created the universe dwells in our hearts . . . and we have to enter our own hearts to discover that Spirit within our own spirit."[28] As arduous as might be that journey to find that place of inner connection to God, the cosmos, and all that is, it is the point of my own regeneration, a dynamism that is waiting to be tapped so as to be my energy, the divine power poured within my heart as my own generative freedom, the capability of co-creating a more human world.

---

[27] *The Essential Rumi,* trans. Coleman Barks (New York: HarperCollins, 1995), 53.

[28] John Main, from *Door to Silence,* quoted in John Main, *Silence and Stillness in Every Season: Daily Readings with John Main,* ed. Paul Harris (New York: Continuum, 2002), 102.

11

Participation

I ended the first chapter describing one of the icons in our chapel. Let me begin this last chapter writing about another one, on the other side of the building. Down a short corridor, in our Mary chapel, there is a beautiful, tender, original rendering of Our Lady of Consolation, created by the same nun. Traced on the floor in front of it (in a very Jungian fashion, unbeknown to me when we designed it) is an isosceles triangle, and then some etched lines coming off the corners, that end in a smaller triangle open to the base of the larger one. The larger triangle represents the Trinity. The smaller triangle is meant to symbolize Mary being assumed into the love life of the Trinity.

Mary was not God. Despite all the popular attempts of the *sensus fidelium* to elevate her as high as possible as the feminine face of the Divine, orthodox teaching is very firm on that. There was rumor that even then-Cardinal Ratzinger felt the need to pull Pope John Paul II back a little in his pronouncements about Mary to make sure that it didn't seem as if she were being elevated to the level of divinity. For me she is a symbol of the human, and more broadly of the body, the earth, and the feminine, being assumed into the love life of the Trinity. At the same time, the tension is good, the longing in us for a feminine face of the Divine. Especially if, as I say, Mary represents not only the feminine but also the body and the earth being brought into right relationship with God as she was always in right relationship.

Perhaps this is the shadow? But the *positive* shadow, the repressed instinctual side trying to come alive. When I speak of the "positive shadow" I always think of two scripture passages: Matthew 10:26, "So have no fear of them; for nothing is covered up that will not be uncovered, and nothing secret that will not become known. What I say to you in the dark, tell in the light; and what you hear whispered, proclaim from the housetops"; and 1 Corinthians 4:5, "Therefore do not pronounce judgment before the time, before the Lord comes, who will bring to light the things now hidden in darkness and will disclose the purposes of the heart."

I regularly mention these three together—the earth, the feminine, and the body—and let's look at some other voices in our tradition who do as well. When he got to the Sistine Chapel in his film series on Catholicism, Bishop Barron spoke about the creation of Eve in Michelangelo's *capolavoro* frescoes on the ceiling. And he points out that in the creation of Adam, God and Adam are both floating in the air. But it's not insignificant that when God creates Eve, both of them have their feet firmly planted on the ground.

Across the cultures the woman's body, especially in connection with childbirth, has long been symbolically associated with earth and materiality and with nature. In the patristic era this became a negative thing: something too closely connected to the earth or the body was considered to be a sin. And so anything female began to be suspect. (Men can only imagine the insult of a woman having to be "churched"—even the Queen of England!—after childbirth, the ultimate icon of the connection of feminine, body, and earth.) But at creation, before the so-called "Fall," Adam and Eve were a balance of matter and spirit, a balance of earth and heaven, and in Michelangelo's depiction, the creation of Eve "is the moment when Spirit and matter cross or, better, when they find their harmony."

In most ancient languages we see hints that the polarity, of mind and matter, for instance, is *complementary* not oppositional, *complementary* not dualistic. It's no accident that the words "matter" and "mother" are closely related to each other, as well as the Greek word for "mother"—*mētēr*. It is also no accident that the Sanskrit root *man-* for "matter" and "mother" is actually the same root as *manas*: mind, mental, and thought.[1] There's a complementarity, not an opposition. They all come from the same root. The Asian traditions bring this into higher relief: consider the yin-yang of Taoism and the sun and moon of *ha-tha* yoga.

Another beautiful image for this trinity of body, earth, and feminine comes from the Buddhist tradition, the Buddha touching the ground just before his enlightenment. The legend is that Siddhartha Gautama, after his years of studying with the ascetics of India, was still not satisfied. So he sat under the Bodhi tree for forty-nine days vowing not to rise until he had attained supreme enlightenment. But the great tempter Mara, the personification of death and the Buddhist equivalent of the Devil, appeared to him right at the end and tried a number of ways to get him to give up his quest. None of Mara's techniques worked, and so in the end Mara just attacked Siddartha's own self-confidence, you might say, insinuating that all of Siddhartha's efforts had been nothing but a self-aggrandizing fantasy. Mara says to him, "You are alone here and you should leave. Who do you have to testify for you?" So Prince Siddhartha reaches down and touches the ground. He calls the earth as his witness.

Up until that moment, you might say that Prince Siddhartha was the epitome of the male spiritual warrior and ascetic. When he touched the earth, he made contact with what is in many traditions

---

[1] The Sanskrit root *man*—"to think" becomes the Greek *menos* and the Latin *mens*, the root of the English "mental." *Mat* is a second root from which come the Sanskrit words *matar* and *matram*. *Matar* becomes the Greek *mētēr* and the Latin *mater* and gives rise to "matter." John Grimes, *A Concise Dictionary of Indian Philosophy*, new and rev. ed. (Varanasi: Indica Books, 2009), 228–229. Jean Gebser adds that *matram*, or "musical instrument," reappears in the Greek *metron*, from which our word "meter" is derived. Jean Gebser, *The Ever-Present Origin*, trans. Noel Barstad with Algis Mickunas (Athens: Ohio University Press, 1985), 76.

understood to be the feminine element. In some accounts of the story a woman actually appears at that moment, a kind of earth goddess. In Thai Buddhist iconography, for instance, there appears a beautiful woman wringing out her long black hair, "releasing floods that wipe away Mara's ten armies." Only when the earth testified for the Buddha could he find liberation.[2]

We have a similar intuition about this in Christianity, specifically personified in Mary. The twelfth-century Cisterican Abbot Saint Amadeus of Lausanne, in a homily on the Virgin, quotes Psalm 72: "*He shall descend like rain upon a fleece, like raindrops on the earth*"; and then he says that "The earth referred to here is the Virgin, who is called earth because of a certain resemblance. Just as the old Adam was formed from untilled earth still free from any disease, so likewise virgin earth produced the new Adam for our world. . . . We have said all this to show that by the word 'earth' we must understand Mary."[3]

Another monastic reference to this same image comes from the Byzantine monk theologian Theodore of Studios, who wrote that "Mary is the land."

She is the land on which the saintly Moses was ordered to take off his sandals as a symbol of the law which was to be superseded by grace. She is the land on which *God who established the earth on its foundations*, as we sing, was established in the flesh by the Spirit. She is the land which without ever being sown nourished God who nourishes all. She is the land on which no thorns of sin ever grew. . . . Blessed is the fruit of the womb of this land.[4]

---

[2]*Buddha Dharma* (Winter 2020): 44. There is also an ancient Buddhist teaching that goes along with this called *yoniso manasikara*. *Yoni* in the Pali/Sanskrit word for "womb," therefore a returning to the womb, returning to the origin.

[3]Huit Homilies Mariales, horn. 3, 2–3: SC 72, 96–102, in *The Word in Season* 1 (December 20): 65.

[4]Homily 3 *in nativitatem*, in *Benedictine Daily Prayer: A Short Breviary, for Common for Feasts of the Blessed Virgin Mary* (Collegeville, MN: Liturgical Press, 2005), 1224.

Remember too Diarmuid O'Murchu's beautiful poetry for this: in and through Mary, "the womb of God and the womb of the universe are one."

The Solemnity of the Assumption of Mary, August 15, was/is also India Independence Day, the day that India gained its independence from England in 1947. I will never be able to forget the connection because of a startling something I learned about the great Indian philosopher and mystic Sri Aurobindo.

Aurobindo Ghosh was a contemporary of Teilhard de Chardin; as a matter of fact, many people speak of them in the same breath, comparing their philosophies. He was born in Calcutta but educated in England. He first turned his prodigious intellect toward a short political career and became a kind of freedom fighter, during which time he became one of the leaders of the movement for the independence from British colonial rule before Gandhi. But then, to make a long story short, he retired to an ashram in the French colony of Pondicherry on the east coast of India on the Bay of Bengal and devoted himself to the development and practice of a new spiritual path which he called "integral yoga." Concerning this integral yoga, whereas in the past the body had been regarded by spiritual seekers as an obstacle, "as something to be overcome and discarded," Aurobindo saw the body instead "as an instrument of spiritual perfection and a field of the spiritual change." Note: not just an *instrument* (not just, as Tertullian would say, a *hinge* of salvation) but the field of transformation, that which gets transformed. He writes, "If a divine life is possible on earth, then this . . . perfection of the body must also be possible."

> The physical consciousness and physical being, the body itself must reach a perfection in all that it is and does which now we can hardly conceive. It may even in the end be suffused with a light and beauty and bliss from the Beyond and the life divine assume a body divine.[5]

---

[5] Sri Aurobindo, *The Supramental Manifestation upon Earth* (Pondicherry: Sri

I slipped that quote into a homily on the Feast of the Transfiguration once. No one knew and no one noticed it had come from an unorthodox—though not heterodox—source.

As it turns out, Aurobindo's birthday was also August 15, and when India finally won its independence, someone wrote to him remarking that wasn't it wonderful that India should have won its independence on his birthday? He replied that it was even more wonderful that India would have won its independence on the feast of the Assumption when a mortal was assumed into the Life Divine, which he thought was the destiny of all humanity. That, of course, was the point of his integral yoga—an evolution to divinity. A yogi might have understood the Assumption better than most Catholics and explained it better and more straightforwardly than most theologians.

QUATERNITY

Now we circle back to Carl Jung. On more than one occurrence, Jung mentioned that the coronation of Mary in heaven endorsed by Pius XII in 1954 in his encyclical *Ad Caeli Reginam* was a most significant "advantage" in Catholicism because that made a quaternity out of the Trinity. He regarded this as a very meaningful *psychological* move. (Remember that Jung thought the Trinity was psychologically unsatisfying and that Christianity had displaced the fourth element.) But recognizing Mary's place not only fulfilled the prophecy in the book of Revelation; it was something that the *sensus fidelium* had held and for which ordinary Catholics had repeatedly pleaded for a long time.

This is Mary as the shadow, the positive shadow, that which got displaced in the unconscious—the earth, the feminine, and the body. Jung explained that Mary, as the instrument of God's birth, "became involved in the Trinitarian drama as a human being." And so the "Mother of God can, therefore, be regarded as a symbol of [humankind's] essential participation in the Trinity."[6] And there it is: Mary as a symbol of humankind, and with it the body and the earth, becoming *involved* (a very careful word) in the drama of the Trinity, the love-life of the Trinity, as a human being. And the other important word is "participation": there is both our participatory consciousness and the idea of not being God by nature, but God by participation. This must have been highly significant for the great psychoanalyst since the frontispiece in volume 11 of Jung's *Collected Works* ("Psychology and Religion West and East") bears a reproduction of a painting by Jean Fouquet titled *The Trinity with the Virgin Mary*.

The German anthropologist Jean Gebser weighed in too, writing that the new dogma of Mary proclaimed by Pope Pius XII could be understood as the "renunciation of the overly emphasized father-aspect of God that is itself a reduction of the divine." He thought that the reinstatement of the maternal principle to its rights and the reduction of the overemphasis on the paternal principle were clear indications that the church was striving for recognition of the whole and integral human person.[7] Putting the accent on the assumption of the *body* also shifts the religious emphasis to the sphere of *transfiguration*. Spiritual *birth* would now be in the foreground, instead of crucifixion and physical death. And Gebser asks, "Will the church of the crucified become the church of the risen? Will Rome adopt the festival of the resurrection or *spiritual birth*, as the more important festival?"[8]

And can we too in our spiritual practice not only prepare ourselves for death and life everlasting in heaven but also access the grace promised to us by our Baptism, Communion, and Confirmation in this life? Will we learn that our flesh is not only the hinge of salvation, but that which can also share in the transformation?

---

[6]Carl Jung, "A Psychological Approach to the Trinity," in *The Collected Works of Carl Jung*, (Princeton, NJ: Princeton University Press), 11:161.

[7]Gebser, *The Ever-Present Origin*, 339–340.

[8]Ibid.

And then, consequently, can we build a spiritual life that embraces and honors all aspects of our being human?

GRACE UPON GRACE

Saint Proclus, a fifth-century theologian, friend and disciple of the great John Chrysostom, insisted on a subtle point concerning the Incarnation of Christ. Christ (Jesus) did not become divine by advancing stages; Christ (the Second Person of the Trinity, Word and Wisdom) was always divine but became human. And so, "We do not preach [Christ as] a deified human being; we confess an incarnate God."[9] Jesus doesn't earn his divinity, work for his divinity, become divine along the way. That's what orthodox Christianity teaches. Jesus was divine all along, even though we could say as a human Jesus grew in grace and strength, and even came to understand the implications of that as a human being would.

But it doesn't end there. Yes, Jesus was not a deified human being; he was God incarnate. But the whole purpose of that Christ event was so that we can be deified human beings. Jesus was the incarnate God, not a deified human being. But we, like Mary, can be deified human beings! That's as good a description of the *telos* of Christian life as any I've heard.

Recall the prologue of the Gospel of John. As we mentioned earlier in discussing Lady Wisdom, the prologue of John is a hymn that seems to have been modeled on older hymns to Wisdom, such as the one in the book of Sirach in which Wisdom praises herself: "I came forth from the mouth of the Most High" (Sir. 24:1ff.). Some scholars see something important about the literary structure of this hymn, that it's built around a chiasm, and the message is hidden in the middle of the hymn. A chiasm has an A-B-C-D-A-B-C scheme. Most of the time when we tell stories, or even jokes,

---

[9]Saint Proclus, *Sermo 1*: ACOI,1, 103–107, in *The Word in Season* 1 (December 25), 206.

the moral or the punch line is at the end. In the parables too the moral meaning is at the end. But in a chiasm, the meaning—the moral—is in the middle. So in the prologue we first hear about the Word and the light (verses 1–5), and then we hear about John the Baptist (verses 7–8), and then we hear that the world did not accept him (verses 9–11). Then comes the punch line, in the middle, which we'll hold off for a moment. Then we hear about the Word again (verses 13–14); and then John the Baptist again (verse 15) and about what happens to those who do accept the Word (verse 16). What's in the middle?

> But to all who receive him, who believed in his name,
> he gave power to become children of God,
> who were born, not of blood or the will of the flesh,
> or human will, but born of God.

That's the center of this hymn, the climax, the main point. This event took place so that *we* could have the power to become children of God. This is what we have said about Jesus the Christ, that he was a Son, a child, an offspring—and we too can be and in some way already are in Christ. St. John tells us in his First Letter, "Beloved, we are God's children now; what we will be has not yet been revealed. What we do know is this: when he is revealed, we will be like him, for we will see him as he is" (1 Jn. 3:2).

The way Abhishiktananda explained it was that Jesus identified with the "I AM" of the Father[10] so we identify with the "I AM" of Jesus. This is echoed in Preface III for the Mass of the Nativity of the Lord:

> . . . through him the holy exchange that restores our life
> shone forth today in splendor:
> when our frailty is assumed by your Word

---

[10]Note the "I AM" statements in the Gospel of John, Jn 4:26; 6:20; 8:24, 28, 58; 13:19; 18:5–6.

not only does human mortality receive unending honor,
by this wondrous union *we, too, are made eternal!*

At the same liturgy, we are treated to this reading from the Letter to the Ephesians. Just as this Word/Sophia was "at play beside
God all the while" (Prov. 8:30), so "God chose us in him before
the world began. . . . God destined us in love to be his children
through Jesus" (Eph. 1:3–6). Just as Paul says that in Jesus "the
fullness of godhead dwelt bodily" and then goes on to say "and
you have come to fullness in him" (Col. 2:9–10), so the prologue
ends (did Paul and John talk this through?) "and from his fullness
we have all received, grace upon grace" (Jn. 1:16).

Grace upon grace? What does that mean? There is already grace
in our having been born, even of blood, even of human will. And
as that great piece of Thomistic theology loves to remind us, *Gratia
non tollit naturam, sed perfecit:* grace does not destroy, but perfects
nature. Grace upon grace!

On the 600th anniversary of the death of Catherine of Siena,
Pope John Paul II, one of the great Christian humanists of the
modern era, said that what we admire in St. Catherine is the same
thing that immediately struck those who approached her—the extraordinary richness of her humanity "that was not dimmed in any
way, but on the contrary [was] increased and perfected by grace."
That made of her "almost a living image of that true and whole-
some Christian humanism," the fundamental law of which he said
was "formulated by Catherine's confrere and teacher," that other
great humanist, "St. Thomas Aquinas, in the well-known aphorism:
'grace builds upon, does not suppress, but presupposes and perfects
nature.'" (John Paul there adds to the pithy original aphorism, in
case we don't grasp the full extent of what it means, and perhaps to
ward off detractors who have a narrow interpretation of it.) "The
person of complete dimensions is the one who is fulfilled in Christ's
grace."[11] Grace, sanctity, the spiritual life, does not diminish us in

---

[11]John Paul II, Apostolic Letter *Amantissima Providentia*, AAS72, April 1980.

any way; rather, our humanity is increased and perfected by grace.

Yes, "Jesus is the reason for the season," but you could equally, justifiably say that *we* are the reason for the season: so that we can become children of God; so that we can identify with the I AM of Jesus, or, in Paul's words, so that we, wild olive shoots that we are, can be grafted on to the vine "to share the richness" (Rom. 11:24); so that (how many times have I quoted this?) "we may share the divinity of Christ who humbled himself to share in our humanity." This is why the ancients liturgically put together the visit of the Magi and the Baptism in the Jordan at the end of the Christmas season with the wedding feast of Cana: the water of our humanity is changed into the wine of divinity. There's the divine alchemy, and it's supposed to be the normal course of things.

Don't miss that point: What I've just described is supposed to be the normal course of things in our lives and in this world of ours.

This is the reason for the season. I don't want to correct Proclus of Constantinople; I just want to finish his thought. Christ did not become divine by advancement; Christ was always divine but became human. So we do not preach Jesus as a deified human being; we confess Jesus as the incarnate God, but a God who became incarnate so that we could become deified human beings. "By this wondrous union we, too, are made eternal."

Don't take my word for it. Listen to John Scotus Eriugena.

It was for this that the Word of God descended into flesh, in order that the flesh, that is, human beings, who through the flesh believe in the Word, might ascend to him, that through the natural, only-begotten Son many might be made adoptive children. It was not for his own sake that the Word became flesh, but for our sake, since only through the flesh of the Word could we be transformed into children of God. He descended alone; he ascends along with many.[12]

English translation published in *L'Osservatore Romano*, weekly edition in English, June 23, 1980, 7.

[12]John Scotus Eriugena, *Sul le Prologe de Jean,* Hom 21–23; in *The Word in Season,*

He ends by saying that the one who made a human being of God makes gods of human beings. It was not for his/her own sake that Word and Wisdom, *Logos-Tao-Sophia*, became flesh, but for our sake. It's not enough for this to be an ephemeral doctrine: we can be transformed into children of God only if the Word and Wisdom of God, the Tao, the *Logos*, was and is made flesh in us.

TWO BECOME ONE

We spent a good deal of time on the first moment of Jesus' life on earth, the Incarnation. Now let's look at the last moment as recorded in the gospels and the Acts of the Apostles, the ascension of Jesus, body and soul, so we teach, to the Father in glory. As John Scotus taught, "He descended alone" but "he ascends along with many."

The ascension of Jesus may be one of the most misunderstood and underappreciated of all the feasts of the Lord that we celebrate in the liturgical year. Part of the reason for that is we fail to realize that that event is about us, too. The authentic teaching of Christianity is that it is *human nature* itself, in the person of Jesus that has been glorified in the Ascension.

Like our *creatio continuo* (creation being an ongoing occurrence), so the ascension of Jesus was the beginning of a whole movement. Jesus is the head of a Body, the fullness of which is the church, "the fullness of him who fills all" (Eph. 1:23). Jesus tells his apostles in his final discourse that "I go now to prepare a place for you . . . so that where I am, you also may be" (Jn. 14:3). Where the head has gone, so will go the rest of the body. Of course, that means the baptized, but let's not forget Cardinal Danielou's teaching about the holy pagans, who make up a part of the church as well. This again is conveyed in the liturgy of the church which proclaims that

vol. I, December 30, 2018. He actually ends with, "The one who made a man of God makes gods of men," which I render with inclusive language in the last sentence.

"the Ascension of Christ your Son is *our* exaltation, and, where the Head has gone before in glory, the Body is called to follow in hope." The Ascension of Christ is *our* telos, our destiny, our end. Let's also not forget that we are part of a larger body as well, that we are the priests of creation that is groaning and in agony while we work this out. We ourselves, as Thomas Berry told us, are "the mystical quality of the Earth."[13] "He descended alone" but "he ascends along with many."

We can circle back to the beginning now and look at the marvelous image of the cloud into which Jesus disappears.[14] That cloud is a symbol both of the great mystery that the Divine is (hence, the darkness of God that Moses entered and the *Cloud of Unknowing*) and an image of the *shekinah*, God's dynamic Spirit who leads the people across the desert and fills the Temple, the temple of Jesus' body, the temple of our bodies. But the angels tell the apostles to stop looking in the sky! Just as Jesus, immediately after his transfiguration (another cloud!)[15] did not wait around to build tents but immediately got right back to mission (all three gospels tell us that coming down the mountain he healed a boy with an unclean spirit), so the apostles too are now commissioned to serve, to participate, to immerse themselves in the world like yeast in the dough, like salt in the earth. The experience of union with God, a vision of God, fills us with the *shekinah* and becomes our power for living as a generative person that has come bursting forth filled with creative energy. The whole of the Christ event unites created reality with uncreated reality. Maximus the Confessor taught: "The two are become one. The whole world enters into the whole of God and by becoming all that God is, except in identity of nature, it received in place of itself the whole God."[16]

---

[13]Plotkin, "Inscendence," 47.

[14]Acts 1:6–11.

[15]Mt. 17:5; Mk. 9:7; Lk. 9:34.

[16]Maximus the Confessor, quoted in Olivier Clement, *The Roots of Christian Mysticism: Texts from the Patristic Era with Commentary*, 2nd ed. (Hyde Park, NY: New City Press, 1993), 54–55.

COMMUNION WITH GOD
THROUGH EARTH

What's the fourth? Everything else is the fourth: the created world, the cosmos in new creation. After all, *God will be all in all.* This is not pantheism, though it may be *pan-en-theism.* What's the difference? Pantheism sees God and the universe as coextensive, meaning that God and universe correspond exactly to each other, even in time and space. Teilhard feared this about his own younger self, especially due to his fascination with stone and other matter. Pan-*en*-theism, however, which is perfectly orthodox, recognizes that God is greater than the universe and the cause and the animating force of the universe, but at the same time God is in (*en-*) the universe and the universe is in God as well. The fourth is the *pan-* ("all") in pan-en-theism. Even if God is more than the sum of all things, all things are a part of God and God is in them all. We're back to Heraclitus's idea that influenced the Stoics, that God the *Logos* pervades the cosmos like a fire.[17]

This is also deification, divinization, everything being brought into right relationship with the Divine until *God will be all in all.*

Teilhard referred to his own early experiences of nature mysticism, as "communion with the earth." That is what he suspected was a kind of pantheistic monism. His suspicion of pantheism later, specifically as he relates it to the inward journey of Eastern mysticism, is that it is too inward, too immanent. At the same time "communion with God" conjured up for him a whole other excess—being too otherworldly, an understanding of God and religion as separate from the world, even anti-world, an exclusive concern for the transcendent, which is how the goal of the spiritual life is too often articulated, as Thomas Berry warned us. That would

---

[17]Heraclitus is quoted as saying something very much like what Jesus himself is reported to have said: "Those who hear not me but the Logos will say: All is one." Jesus in the Gospel of John claims, "The word you hear is not mine, but it is from the Father who sent me," and "The Father and I are one" (Jn. 14:24, 10:30).

be a spirituality that does not place enough importance on the value of human effort and the development of the world, a theme Teilhard developed extensively in *The Divine Milieu.*

As Ursula King describes Teilhard's journey, both of these attitudes—communion with earth and communion with God—are incomplete. What we are looking for is a synthesis of both, not, however, "as a simple combination of two attractions but as something of a new order altogether." And so she suggests that "communion with God *through* earth"—through flesh, through matter, through creation—is the best way to describe Teilhard's lifelong attempt "to relate God and the world in the most intimate manner," as shown through his efforts at seeing science and religion as part of the same quest for ultimate unity, and also in relating mystical spirituality to effort and action.[18]

The British iconographer Aidan Hart asks, "Why has God made us of matter as well as of spirit? Why has God placed us in a world full of density? Are we supposed to struggle through it until we emerge into the world of pure spirit? Is the material world an obstruction, or the result of some ghastly mistake as the gnostics might lead us to believe? Is the soul trapped in the body as in a tomb as the Platonists would have us believe?" He answers his own question with the knowledge that fires Christian artists and ecologists, because these are important questions not only for sacred art but for our dealings with the environment as well. And the answer is that none of the above is adequate for a Christian understanding of the relation of the One to the many, of God to creation. For us the material world is an essential part of our calling to become *partakers of the divine nature*, creation is an essential part of our becoming "gods by grace," as the writers of the patristic era put it. And the Christian answer is also a call to duty: matter is created by God, is good, and is part of the divine plan for *our* deification.[19]

---

[18]Ursula King, *Towards a New Mysticism: Teilhard de Chardin and Eastern Religions* (New York: Seabury Press, 1981), 29–30.

[19]Aidan Hart, *Beauty-Spirit-Matter: Icons in the Modern World* (Leominster, UK: Gracewing, 2014), 80–81.

Yes, we believe that the material world has been sullied by the Fall; the relationship has been disrupted. Indeed, if you read the story in Genesis carefully, *all* relationships have been disrupted by the disruption of the relationship with God: the relationship between male and female; their relationships with their own bodies; and their relationship with the earth. All has become subject to decay.

But we have a new Adam: Jesus the Christ, Word and Wisdom made flesh. And we have a new Eve: Mary, mother of Jesus, who births God into the world of matter. And a new garden: the garden of the resurrection. The promise of Christianity is that *God will be all in all*. We still believe that matter per se is created and blessed by God and that through grace it can become like Moses's bush, which burned with God's fire (is this the permeating fire of Heraclitus's *logos?*) without being consumed by it. Everything can become—and in some way already is—a vessel to hold God's energy, like Jesus at his transfiguration, and the promise for our own bodies as well. This is our "tantric" sacramental view of creation. As we sing every day at the Eucharist in the words of the prophet Isaiah, "Holy, holy, holy Lord God of hosts: heaven *and* earth are full of your glory."

THE HEART OF THE WORLD

There is our Fourth Dimension—the Dance. None of this ever just takes us away to heaven, but it also returns us to Earth in a new way. Back to Earth recognizing "our role as an integral member of the earth community" with a truly humanistic rather than radically anthropocentric attitude, one that recognizes that to remain viable we as a species "must establish a niche for ourselves that is beneficial both for [ourselves] and for [our] surrounding community,"[20] of which we are the priests and the servant leaders.

---

[20]Thomas Berry, *The Dream of the Earth* (San Francisco: Sierra Club Books, 1990), 209.

My teacher Bruno was not fond of ladders and staircases, especially those specious ones that lead the monks away from earth and up to heaven. He preferred the approach of Teilhard and Jung, and the wisdom of the primal peoples. This phrase of Jung is particularly telling: "the dark weight of the earth." Here is how that dark weight of the earth leads us to the cross (this is Bruno quoting Jung): If God is born as a human being and wants to unite humankind in the fellowship of the Spirit, then God "must suffer the horrible torture of having to endure the world in all its reality. This is the cross that [God] has to bear, and he himself is the cross. The whole world is God's suffering, and every individual . . . who wants to get anywhere near their own wholeness knows that this is the way of the cross."[21] Our cross, our kenosis, is our dying to our separateness so as to move from individual to person and join in the dance of *all in all.*

This is why the cross is a universal, archetypal symbol: at the top, the source, the Silence, the Father, the Mother, the One; one arm is the Word and Wisdom, Tao, Sophia, Logos—for us, Jesus, the Offspring; the other arm is the Spirit, the dynamism, the *shekinah, shakti-kundalini, chi,* the Music. But we must never forget this fourth all-important direction which is rooted in the ground—the Incarnation. This Fourth Movement is intimately tied up with Christ's *kenosis,* emptying and diminishment that precedes the resurrection, and John the Baptist's "I must decrease and Christ must increase," the action of the eucharistic energy, and our being broken open and poured for the sake of the world.

As we sing in an Easter hymn, that's when "the cross deep-rooted breaks in bloom / as all is gathered into Christ."

As we end our meditation on this fourth element, our participation, we might reflect on how our own spirituality and our actual spiritual practices reflect—or do not reflect—this holistic view: grace builds on but does not destroy nature. Do we consider our own bodies and the earth as part of our spiritual life? The conversion

---

[21]Bruno Barnhart, *The Future of Wisdom* (New York: Continuum, 2007), 151.

experience, if I may use that phrase, came for me when I realized that everything I do can be a part of my spiritual life, a spiritual practice. My entire lifestyle now comes under spiritual discernment, care for my own physical well-being, understanding my body really as a temple of the Spirit, even physical exercise and proper diet become integral elements of my spiritual life and a celebration of my being a participant in the divine nature. And if I realize my relatedness to creation, gardening and hiking, along with any attention to ecological concerns through conscious consuming and recycling, now become spiritual practices. I myself and the piece of earth I inhabit become the beginning of the new heaven and the new earth, because I myself am a new creation. In the words of Sri Aurobindo, all of life becomes to me "at once a revelation and a fine trysting place."[22]

[22]Sri Aurobindo, *The Synthesis of Yoga* (Pondicherry: All India Books, 1986), 566.

Conclusion

Everything Is Holy Now

My last real conversation with Bruno Barnhart, just two days before he died, was about Bede Griffiths. Bruno said we need a new
Bede Griffiths, but, he said, "Maybe the next Bede Griffiths won't
be a Bede Griffiths. Maybe it will be a woman. Maybe a mother,
someone who lives entirely in someone else, giving her life away,
more hidden than Jesus." Like a seed that falls into the ground and
dies, like yeast in the dough, like salt in the earth, that works by
disappearing. The reign of God is like that, you know.

When I started this whole project, I had no "feminist agenda,"
meaning, I didn't have as one of my goals to bring out the feminine
dimension of the Divine. She just kept showing up! That aspect
simply unfolded more and more the deeper I dug into the mystery
of the Trinity—God as the Great Mother, Sophia, and *shekinah*-
energy, and finally Mary as the icon and enfleshment of the body,
the earth and the feminine. And it seemed to me obvious that this
dimension is essential for the evolution of our consciousness in
our understanding of the Divine since, again, the feminine is so
closely aligned with the body and the earth.

Some years ago, a friend sent me a song called "Holy Now" that
she thought I would enjoy. I listened dutifully, but I actually found
the song kind of offensive. It seemed as if the singer-songwriter
was poking fun at Catholicism, or at least making light of the
sacraments. The first verse was about going to church on Sunday

where the priest would "read the holy words" and "consecrate the holy bread." But today, he sang, "the only difference is / *everything is holy now.*"[1] So, I just ignored the song and forgot about it. Then one day I happened upon the song again, and it struck me in a whole different way. He wasn't putting down the Eucharist; he was just saying that we are eventually meant to see holiness everywhere. At that point, "the challenging thing becomes / not to look for miracles / but finding where there isn't one." I started singing that song myself very often, introducing it by explaining that I thought this was actually one of the fundamental *raisons d'être* of monastic life. Saint Benedict says that even the tools of the monastery ought to be treated as if they were vessels for the altar. And when speaking of the discipline of psalmody, Benedict says that indeed we believe that the divine presence of God is everywhere.[2]

My favorite line of the song comes in the third verse: "This morning outside I stood / and saw a little red-winged bird / shining like a burning bush / and singing like a scripture verse." There were times when I would, to my embarrassment, have to stop singing because I would be so moved by that image that I would choke up with tears and couldn't get the words out. The songwriter, Peter Mayer, actually aligns himself with Maximus the Confessor's teaching on the transfiguration of Jesus, saying that the Christ event unites created reality with uncreated reality: "the two are become one. The whole world enters into the whole of God and by becoming all that God is, except in identity of nature, it received in place of itself the whole God."[3] First, Jesus becomes the burning bush on the mount of transfiguration; then *we* do, and then all of creation becomes like that burning bush, a vessel holding divinity.

We are speaking here too of that final moment or, rather, the

---

[1]One reference in the lyric does still strike me as too flippant, when he sings "Wine from water is not so small / But an even better magic trick / Is that anything is here at all." I like the sentiment, but I change "magic trick" to "miracle" when I sing it.

[2]Benedict's *Rule* 31:10–11; 19:1. Translation mine.

[3]Maximus the Confessor, quoted in Olivier Clement, *The Roots of Christian Mysticism: Texts from the Patristic Era with Commentary,* 2nd ed. (Hyde Park, NY: New City Press, 1993), 54–55.

culminating moment, the *telos*, when *God will be all in all*, as Bruno wrote, "When, in the resurrection, our body participates fully in this change," and "a transformation by the Holy Spirit will be complete."[4] But a transformation not only in ourselves! And Bruno then goes back to a phrase that he and I spoke about often—and I have already quoted so many times—from Paul to the Romans: "For the creation waits with eager longing for the revealing of the children of God . . . the whole creation has been groaning . . . while we wait for adoption, the redemption of our bodies" (8:19–23). All of creation, all of the cosmos, is waiting in a kind of expectant agony while we human beings, the priests of creation, work this out in our own flesh. This is our duty, our place in the hierarchy, if you will.

This is also the Christian mystical vision at its most refined, and a Christian understanding of nonduality: our redemption—body and soul—becomes yeast in the dough of the earth and one small part of a movement of all creation coming into right relationship with God, and *God will be all in all*—Panikkar's cosmotheandric: God, the cosmos, and the human person in a great perichoresis. "At last all things are made new—new song, new name, new Jerusalem, new heaven and earth. Not by annihilation of the old, but by taking it all up, at last into the divine union."[5]

There is a beautiful story in the *Life of Benedict* as told by Saint Gregory the Great in his *Dialogues*. This is near the end of Benedict's life. Gregory has already told us that Benedict had watched his sister Scholastica's soul leave her body and enter the court of heaven; and right after this he saw the soul of his friend Germanus "being carried by angels up to heaven in a ball of fire." In a sense we are seeing Benedict preparing for his own death, and perhaps in some way it is a culminating vision of his whole life's journey; we could call it a unitive vision. And then one day:

---

[4]Ibid., 49.

[5]Cyril C. Martindale, "Saint John and the Apocalypse," quoted *in The Word in Season*, vol. 3, Friday, Fourth Week of Easter (Villanova, PA: Augustinian Press, 2001), 69.

In the dead of the night he suddenly beheld a flood of light shining down from above more brilliant than the sun, and with it every trace of darkness cleared away. . . . According to his own description, the whole world was gathered up before his eyes in what appeared to be a single ray of light.[6]

Remembering N. T. Wright's admonition that God is not all in all *yet* until the final victory over evil and death, lest we wind up colluding with them . . . Still, there are moments, aren't there? When it all seems to come together and reveal itself in its reality. There's a teaching in the Soto Zen tradition of the difference between *satori* and *kensho*. If I understand it correctly, *satori* is sort of a permanent state of enlightenment that one can reach, whereas *kensho* is a flash, a glimpse, like a peek at the Beloved in the garden that keeps the Bride longing. There are these *kensho* moments that stand out in the midst of the ordinary, perhaps when we really see and hear that red-winged bird, or we "see another new morning come" or "a questioning child's face," and catch a glimpse of what Reality really is and is meant to be, "already and not yet," as we say about the Reign of God.

In conclusion allow me to iterate and adapt one last time the meditation of Tauler that we met at the beginning. "It is much better to have experience of the Trinity than to talk about it," he wrote. "We should learn to find the Trinity in ourselves, and realize how we are in a real way formed according to its image. If we want to experience this we must turn inward, away from the activities of our faculties, both exterior and interior, away from all imaginations and all the notions we have acquired from outside ourselves"— hopefully this is the exercise that we have done in these preceding pages—"and sink and lose ourselves in the depths." It is then that

---

[6]Gregory the Great, *Life and Miracles of St. Benedict* #35 (Collegeville, MN: Liturgical Press), 71.

the power of the Silence will come,
the Silence which is also a font of Being
and the womb of the Great Mother.

And this Silence will call the soul into Itself
through *Logos* and *Sophia*, the Word and Wisdom,
and just as Word and Wisdom, Sophia and the *Tao*,
are born of the Silence and return to Silence,
so we are born of Silence in Wisdom
and flow back into the Silent Source
through Word and Wisdom,
becoming one with them.
And when that happens . . .

the Music of the Spirit pours itself out,
as energy, in dynamism,
in unspeakable and overflowing love and joy,
flooding and saturating the depths of our soul with pre-
    cious gifts.
And then of course, comes the dance—
and we *are* the dance,
and all of creation that is groaning
while we work out this redemption of our bodies.

Lady Wisdom in Scripture

Proverbs 8:22–33

The Lord created me at the beginning of his work,
the first of his acts of long ago.
Ages ago I was set up,
at the first,
before the beginning of the earth.
When there were no depths
I was brought forth,
when there were no springs abounding with water.
Before the mountains had been shaped,
before the hills, I was brought forth—
when he had not yet made earth and fields,
or the world's first bits of soil.
When he established the heavens,
I was there,
when he drew a circle on the face of the deep,
when he made firm the skies above,
when he established the fountains of the deep,
when he assigned to the sea its limit,
so that the waters might not transgress his command,
when he marked out the foundations of the earth,
then I was beside him,
like a master worker;

and daily I was his delight,
rejoicing before him always,
rejoicing in his inhabited world
and delighting in the human race.

"And now, listen to me, my children:
Happy are those who keep my ways.
Hear instruction and be wise,
and do not neglect it.
Happy is the one who listens to me,
watching daily at my gates,
waiting beside my doors.
For whoever finds me finds life
and obtains favor from the Lord."

Proverbs 9:1–6
Wisdom has built her house,
she has hewn her seven pillars.
She has slaughtered her animals,
she has mixed her wine,
she has also set her table.
She has sent out her servant-girls,
she calls from the highest places in the town:
"You that are simple, turn in here!"
To those without sense she says,
"Come, eat of my bread
and drink of the wine I have mixed.
Lay aside immaturity, and live,
and walk in the way of insight."

Sirach 24:1–9; 19–21
Wisdom praises herself,
and tells of her glory in the midst of her people.
In the assembly of the Most High she opens her mouth,
and in the presence of his hosts she tells of her glory:

"I came forth from the mouth of the Most High,
and covered the earth like a mist.
I dwelt in the highest heavens,
and my throne was in a pillar of cloud.
Alone I compassed the vault of heaven
and traversed the depths of the abyss.
Over waves of the sea, over all the earth,
and over every people and nation I have held sway.
Among all these I sought a resting place;
in whose territory should I abide?
"Then the Creator of all things gave me a command,
and my Creator chose the place for my tent.
He said, 'Make your dwelling in Jacob,
and in Israel receive your inheritance.'
Before the ages, in the beginning, he created me,
and for all the ages I shall not cease to be.

"Come to me, you who desire me,
and eat your fill of my fruits.
For the memory of me is sweeter than honey,
and the possession of me sweeter than the honeycomb.
Those who eat of me will hunger for more,
and those who drink of me will thirst for more."

Acknowledgments

Particular thanks to the Benedictine women of Saint Scholastica Monastery, Mount Angel, Oregon, for whom these chapters were originally organized as a retreat; to the Episcopal House of Prayer, Collegeville, Minnesota, and participants in the online conferences of the same; to my brother monks of New Camaldoli Hermitage, who patiently allowed me to think through this material out loud in countless homilies and chapter conferences; and to the faithful members of Sangha Shantivanam of Santa Cruz, California, for their ever-enthusiastic receptivity and desire to learn about the experience of Absolute Reality as found in all the world's spiritual traditions, with particular mention of Sr. Barbara Long, OP, and Gitanjali Lori Rivera for small but precious contributions on Pseudo-Dionysius and Catherine of Siena, and the Sufi understanding of *fanā*, respectively. I am so grateful for all my precious amazing friends, especially John Marheineke and Andrew Nguyen for patiently listening to my excited disjointed musings during long walks on the beach and hikes in the hills; to Fede, Claire and Nick, Br. Timothy Jolley, OHC, and Sr. Donald Corcoran, OSB Cam. for reading through early drafts. My deep gratitude to Robert Ellsberg and Jon Sweeney for inviting me to join the august ranks of Orbis authors and for amazing editorial care. Finally, a deep bow of respect to my elders, especially Bede Griffiths, Bruno Barnhart, and Raimundo Panikkar, whose legacy of rearticulating the truths of our faith with new ardor, new methods, and new language I, however inadequately, wish to preserve and continue. May we all stay close to Lord Jesus in—and make him known through—the Wisdom of the Word and the Breaking of the Bread.